PRAISE FOR *TRULY FREE*

"Robert Morris has a remarkable way of knowing where I live and helping me move forward. His common sense is anything but common. It, and he, are gifts of God. I love him and his teaching."

—MAX LUCADO
PASTOR AND AUTHOR

"*Truly Free* is a great reminder that there is a spiritual battle raging all around us, but we have the victory in Christ. This book can give you hope no matter what struggles you are facing."

—JOYCE MEYER
BIBLE TEACHER AND BESTSELLING AUTHOR

"*Truly Free* points the way to a literal unshackling from mental torment, self-destructive habits, unperceived hindrances of pride, unforgiveness, and secret sins—opening the doorway God's Word provides for fullness of liberty, in mind, soul, thoughts, habits, and emotions. Here is a Christ-centered, thoroughly Word-based case for, and a God-given pathway into, freedom. *Truly Free* is a patient unfolding of biblical studies that reveal the Savior's kingdom's power over all that is demonic, deceiving, or destructive of human wholeness."

—PASTOR JACK W. HAYFORD
CHANCELLOR, THE KING'S UNIVERSITY; AND FOUNDING
PASTOR, THE CHURCH ON THE WAY

"It's rare to meet anyone who doesn't battle with some reoccurring sins or destructive thought patterns. That's why Pastor Robert's new book, *Truly Free*, is a must-read for anyone who is tired of feeling trapped in a destructive cycle. Pastor Robert's honesty is disarming; his suggestions are practicable; but most importantly, his spiritual insights are life transforming. I hope you will read this book and become *truly free*.

—CRAIG GROESCHEL
SENIOR PASTOR, LIFECHURCH.TV; AND AUTHOR, *FROM THIS DAY
FORWARD: FIVE COMMITMENTS TO FAIL-PROOF YOUR MARRIAGE*

"No successful person can walk through life without confronting the issues that hold him or her back. If you want to go to the next level in your relationships in your job, and in your relationship with God, then you are going to have to identify what is holding you back. Robert Morris's principles and advice will help you start your journey to being *truly free*."

—JOHN C. MAXWELL
BESTSELLING AUTHOR

"This book is filled with liberating truths every believer needs to know. Robert is so gifted at simplifying the Bible and making it practical. *Truly Free* isn't just a great book—it is a spiritual experience that will deepen your relationship with Christ and set you free to live as God intended."

—JIMMY EVANS
FOUNDER AND CEO, MarriageToday

"I am so thankful for the honesty and boldness of Robert Morris in his book *Truly Free*. Sharing his own story and practical advice for how he broke free from his personal battles is inspiring. Anyone who has ever struggled with overcoming the chains of sin in his or her life should absolutely read this book!"

—PERRY NOBLE
SENIOR PASTOR, NewSpring CHURCH; AND
AUTHOR, *Unleash!* AND *Overwhelmed*

"Right in the Lord's Prayer, Jesus teaches us to pray: 'Lead us not into temptation, but deliver us from evil.' In His parable of the sower, He pictures Satan coming quickly to *snatch away* the good seed. Clearly, we're in a battle, folks—in our minds and emotions as well as for our eternal spirits—and the enemy is not just our flesh but the devil himself. Robert Morris reveals the nature of the struggle we all face and the sure ways to win. Every believer needs to read this book."

—PAT BOONE
CHRISTIAN ACTIVIST AND ENTERTAINER

TRULY FREE

TRULY FREE

Breaking the Snares That So Easily Entangle

ROBERT MORRIS

W Publishing Group

An Imprint of Thomas Nelson

Published in Nashville, Tennessee, by W Publishing Group, an imprint of Thomas Nelson.

Published in association with the literary agency of Winters & King, Inc.

Thomas Nelson titles may be purchased in bulk for educational, business, fund-raising, or sales promotional use. For information, please e-mail SpecialMarkets@ThomasNelson.com.

Unless otherwise indicated, Scripture quotations are taken from the New King James Version®. © 1982 by Thomas Nelson, Inc. Used by permission. All rights reserved.

Scripture quotations marked NIV are taken from the Holy Bible, New International Version®, NIV®. © 1973, 1978, 1984, 2011 by Biblica, Inc.™ Used by permission of Zondervan. All rights reserved worldwide.

Scripture quotations marked ESV are taken from the English Standard Version. © 2001 by Crossway Bibles, a division of Good News Publishers.

Scripture quotations marked NASB are from New American Standard Bible®. © The Lockman Foundation 1960, 1962, 1963, 1968, 1971, 1972, 1973, 1975, 1977, 1995. Used by permission.

Scripture quotation marked NLT is from Holy Bible, New Living Translation. © 1996, 2004, 2007. Used by permission of Tyndale House Publishers, Inc., Wheaton, Illinois 60189. All rights reserved.

Scripture quotation marked WEB is from the World English Bible™. Public domain.

Scripture quotations marked KJV are taken from the King James Version. Public domain.

Italics added to Scripture quotations are the author's own emphasis.

ISBN 978-0-7180-3580-8 (IE)

Library of Congress Cataloging-in-Publication Data

Morris, Robert, 1961 July 29-
  Truly free : breaking the snares that so easily entangle / Robert Morris.
     pages cm
  Includes bibliographical references.
  ISBN 978-0-7180-1110-9 (hardcover)
  1. Christian life. 2. Peace of mind. 3. Liberty—Religious aspects—Christianity. I. Title.
  BV4501.3.M6738 2015
  248.4—dc23

2014036310

Printed in the United States of America

15 16 17 18 19 RRD 6 5 4 3 2 1

CONTENTS

CONTENTS

This book is dedicated to my beautiful wife, Debbie, who has walked with me through struggles and triumphs for more than thirty-five years.

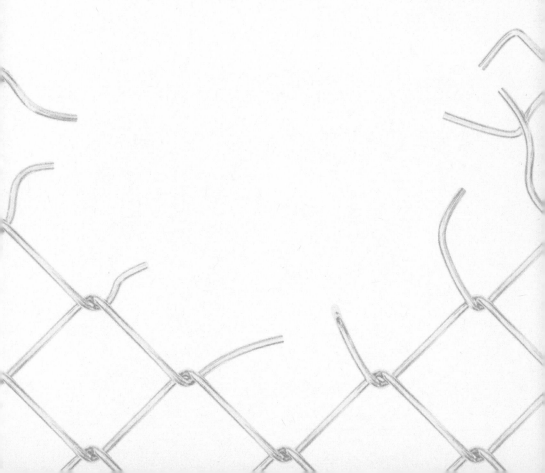

Introduction

FREE AT LAST

It is for freedom that Christ has set us free.
Stand firm, then, and do not let yourselves be
burdened again by a yoke of slavery.

—GALATIANS 5:1 NIV

Their forgetfulness began in earnest on the fifteenth day of the second month of their new calendar. Out in the desert, however, most folks didn't bother to keep count of what day it was.

Mostly, everybody just noticed their sweat—how everybody stank the same bad way. They noticed the sand as it wedged its way into their sandals and between their toes and drifted into their eyes and nostrils with each step they took. They noticed the heat—how breath after breath, the desert air burned in their lungs.

The Israelites were hitting the wall of desert reality.

Already the cool water and palm trees of the oasis of Elim lay far behind them. The relief of shade from Mount Sinai lay in the shadowy distance. The promised land seemed so far ahead of them, they wondered if they'd ever arrive.

All that stench and heat and dust and desert grime mixed together proved the perfect climate to birth forgetfulness. As recorded in Exodus 16, the grumblings on that fifteenth day of the second month since coming out of Egypt started out something like this:

"Hey." An Israelite wiped the sweat off his forehead. "What I wouldn't give right now to be back sitting in the shade of my old house."

"Yeah," said another, a faraway look in her eyes. "We really had it good back there, didn't we?"

A third chimed in. "Back in Egypt we sat around pots of meat and ate all the food we wanted. Remember all those fresh onions and garlic and leeks? So tasty!"

They felt their mouths water, even in the arid heat.

And from there the grumbling erupted.

How Bad It Really Was

Did you catch what important truth the Israelites had forgotten?

They'd been slaves!

The Israelites had escaped bondage in Egypt through the power of God, but in the wilderness they were still imprisoned by their selective memory of life in Egypt.

Back in Egypt they might have eaten fresh onions and garlic and leeks on rare occasions. But they had also labored from dawn to dusk every day under the unbending orders that they make bricks without straw. Egypt came complete with cruel taskmasters and whips and chains and shackles and wrenching poverty. All their baby boys had once been thrown into the Nile River.

Repeatedly—desperately—the Israelites had cried out to God for a deliverer.

Now they'd forgotten they had been in bondage.

They'd also forgotten that God had answered their cry. God had sent a deliverer to lead them out of slavery.

But hold on a moment. Before we come down too hard on the Israelites, have you ever considered how susceptible we are today to do or at least lean toward the same thing?

This Present Egypt

If we're Christians, then the Lord has delivered us out of slavery. Through Christ's work on the cross, Jesus has removed our despair and darkness and put in its place victory, strength, and freedom. The old is gone. The new has come. We are a new creation (2 Corinthians 5:17). We never need to return to Egypt.

And yet . . .

A life of slavery still beckons to us. We find that our old, harmful thoughts are hard to shake. Our former, unhealthy habits are hard to break. Long-embedded patterns of shameful living continue to entangle us—day after day, month after month, even year after year.

Some days we feel weighed down by those shackles. We long for the freedom to respond to God fully as the people He has created and redeemed us to be. But fear and heaviness and darkness surround us. We wonder where to turn.

We need to recognize the reality and presence of the spiritual realm. We need to step fully into God's plan to heal our broken world. We need to move into life and healing, purity, liberty, holiness, and truth.

But how?

Finally Free

In the pages ahead, I want to explore with you a glorious truth—that the promise of being delivered from our slavery is a promise to be set free *completely*.

Forget Egypt. You don't ever want to return to your personal Egypt.

The reality of being truly free is one you may not have explored fully before. A big problem for us is that evil still exists in the world today. Christ has conquered sin and death, yes, but in His infinite wisdom— for reasons that are often difficult for us to understand—the effects of evil are still permitted to exist. We can still be influenced by evil. We can still be oppressed by evil. We can even be controlled by evil. Even if we're saved.

In the chapters to come we are going to surface a need you may not have known you had. At this very moment there is scriptural evidence that you and I can be negatively influenced by evil. That same evil can entrap us and harm us, oppress us and hurt us, and generally make our lives difficult, even enslave us to harmful patterns of living we thought we had left behind.

But we don't want to dwell on evil in this book. You won't hear prolonged stories of the bizarre, the cruel and unusual, or the weird. I won't tell any stories that keep you awake at night or stories that sound as though they're pulled from the tabloids.

Instead, I want to dwell on the goodness and power and truth of Jesus Christ. That's what this book is all about: how God sets us free. All authority has been given to Jesus (Matthew 28:18). He has conquered death, hell, and evil (1 Corinthians 15:54–56). He now reigns at God's right hand and will reign forevermore (Acts 2:33).

The good news is that regardless of what difficulty you're struggling with today, there is always hope. Sure, the temptation never quite goes away in this life. There is always a pull toward thoughts and actions that could cause us to become burdened again by a yoke of slavery (Galatians 5:1 NASB). But you need to know—and live out fully—that you never need to return to Egypt. With Jesus Christ, you can be free at last, free forever, truly and finally free.

If that sounds like something you long for, I invite you to keep reading.

—Robert Morris
Dallas, Texas

Chapter One

GREATER IS HE

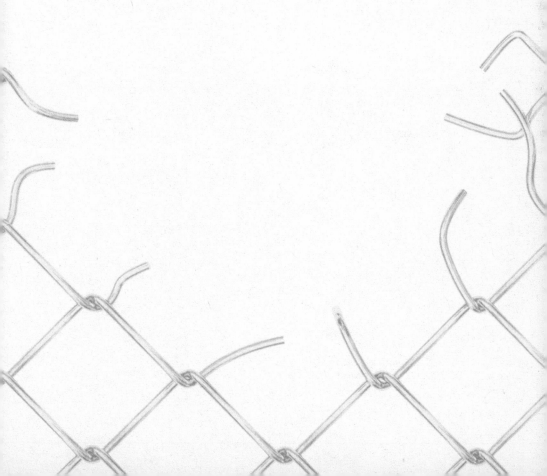

For we do not wrestle against flesh and blood,
but . . . against spiritual hosts of
wickedness in the heavenly places.

—EPHESIANS 6:12

My wife, Debbie, and I are building a house right now. It's on some land we recently purchased in the country. The construction workers have been really good about welcoming us to the site whenever we come by to check on progress, and it's been exciting to watch a dream take shape from the ground up.

On one visit to the site, however, we had a little incident involving an animal. Now, I'm a big fan of animals. Dogs, cats, horses, giraffes, zebras, chimpanzees. I loved going to the zoo when I was a kid, and I appreciate a good household pet as a grownup. But there are some animals that give me a hard time. Out in the wild—fine. Live and let live. But inside my house or anywhere near the people I love—then watch out.

Usually anywhere within the city limits of the Dallas–Fort Worth Metroplex where we currently live, you're fine. But drive anywhere outside town, and you'll soon see that Texas is the land of fire ants, tarantulas, and—you guessed it—rattlesnakes.

So the other day Debbie and I were out visiting the construction site. The foundation was poured, the floors were roughed in, and the framing was finished, but that was it. Our house was wide-open to the wilds. As we were walking around the work site, Debbie suddenly stopped.

"Robert!" she said. "Quick—look over there!"

Sure enough, not far from where my wife stood, a rattlesnake lay coiled on the floor of my future home. It was easy to see why he had come inside. A workman had left part of his lunch lying around—a hard-boiled egg—and the rattlesnake had slid up with a smile on his face to take a bite.

What would you do in that situation?

Now, remember: I'm an animal lover. Live and let live. But I'm also a Texas boy at heart. If I find a tarantula lurking in my bathroom sink, I don't try to make friends with him. The same goes for rattlesnakes. I have young grandchildren, and I don't want a brood of venomous serpents anywhere near my house.

A rattlesnake is actually a pit viper, *not* a kind snake. He's introverted and likes to be left alone, and usually he'll only strike when threatened. But if a rattler does strike—and he *will* strike if given the right opportunity—he has enough venom in his fanged bite to inflict serious harm, even kill a person.

What did I do?

I grabbed the nearest two-by-four, walked over, and bashed that snake in the head.

Spiritual Snakes

Guess what? This same kind of problem confronts a lot of people. Unwelcome snakes of the spiritual sort can slither into our houses, particularly when doors and windows are left wide-open. Those spiritual snakes are dangerous. They're not to be treated as friends. They need to be shown the door out.

Even though this is the subject we want to deal with in this book, I realize the idea of spiritual snakes can make some people uncomfortable. So I want to begin this entire discussion with a scripture I pray you'll drill into your mind and never let go of. It's found in 1 John 4:4: "He who is in you is greater than he who is in the world."

God is greater!

That's what this book is ultimately about. God is always greater. Thanks to God, we have nothing to fear.

Why am I so confident of that? It's because I believe a simple, straightforward truth.

A while back a friend of mine traveled to Haiti. It's a country of deep poverty and widespread occult practices. The missionary with whom my friend stayed told him how he and others had started a new church in one of the villages. The only land they could find to purchase for the church building was right next door to a witch doctor.

"Wow," the friend said. "Weren't you afraid?"

The missionary casually examined the back of his fingernails. He looked almost bored. "Nah," he said. "We have Christ."

That's the straightforward truth. As believers, *we have Christ!* We never need to be afraid. Yet it's also true that believers are not immune to the effects of evil. That's uncomfortable to think about, I know. But we will never achieve the levels of peace, joy, and effectiveness to which we are called if we're being influenced by evil in certain compartments of our lives. And if we're leaders in the church, then it's very difficult to lead God's people in freedom if we're not modeling a lifestyle of liberty ourselves.

Do you have any area of your life where you simply can't get victory? Is there a sin that you've confessed over and over and over again? You've told God, "I'll never do that again," but you keep doing it. Do you consistently struggle with depression, anger, lust, discontentment, resentment, bitterness, jealousy, or despair?

The influence of spiritual evil is more common than we think. Spiritual snakes can slither into the open doors and windows of our lives. They need to be dealt with. We need to grapple with this idea that spiritual oppression can happen to anyone.

Even you and me.

We Have Christ

The Bible shows that the devil is real, and Ephesians 6:10–13 exhorts us:

> Be strong in the Lord and in the power of His might. Put on the whole
> armor of God, that you may be able to stand against the wiles of the
> devil. For we do not wrestle against flesh and blood, but against
> principalities, against powers, against the rulers of the darkness of
> this age, against spiritual hosts of wickedness in the heavenly places.
> Therefore take up the whole armor of God, that you may be able to
> withstand in the evil day, and having done all, to stand.

Notice that we are called to "wrestle . . . against spiritual hosts of
wickedness." That's a key concept. Spiritual attacks are real, and they
can wreak havoc on people's lives today. But we don't need to lose these
spiritual wrestling matches because Christ is our wrestling coach. Jesus
saves us. Jesus frees us. He trains us to resist the power of evil and delivers
us from anything that can hold us back.

All power and authority has been given to Jesus (Matthew 28:18),
and He wants to release us from spiritual oppression. That's good news.
Freedom is available for us today. But we will never get free if we don't
know we're in bondage in the first place. We need to know that the
problem of evil spiritual influence is very real.

In light of that, there's a word we need to talk about. I realize even
the word can make people shudder, but it's a biblical word, so let's not
shy away from it. The word is *demons*.

Sometimes people talk about demons in a metaphoric sense. They'll
speak of a famous singer who has "conquered his demons"—usually
some kind of bad habit—and now is back on top of the charts. Or you
hear a person say, "Yeah, I've got to get this demon off my back," meaning
he needs to conquer some sort of problem.

This is not how the Bible uses the term *demon*. In Mark 5, an example is given of a literal unclean spirit who had taken up residence inside a person's body. Jesus and His disciples were traveling by boat on the Sea of Galilee. They came to the south side of the lake, pulled their boat onshore in "the country of the Gadarenes" (v. 1), and were immediately confronted by a naked man running around a cemetery. Not a pretty picture, but that's how the Bible describes him.

The disciples asked around and discovered that the man had actually been living among the tombs. Imagine it—those dark places were where the man slept at night and ate his meals. Day and night he cried out and cut himself with stones. He exhibited dangerous behavior and even supernatural strength. The people of the region had tried to bind him with shackles and chains, yet he had pulled apart the chains and broken the shackles.

When this man saw Jesus from afar, he ran straight toward Jesus, bowed down to Him, and cried out in a loud voice, "What have I to do with You, Jesus, Son of the Most High God? I implore You by God that You do not torment me" (v. 7).

Clearly the demon was speaking through the man. (Jesus wouldn't torment a man.) And Jesus answered simply, "Come out of the man, unclean spirit" (v. 8).

They talked some more, and the demon revealed his name— Legion, a Roman term that referred to a group of 6,826 soldiers. In other words, more than one demon was afflicting the man. The demons begged not to be sent away. They wanted to stay where they already had established a stronghold. So Jesus gave the demons permission to enter a herd of pigs feeding nearby. The demons came out of the man and entered the pigs, which ran violently down a hill into the sea, where they drowned.

When the people of the region heard about the incident, they hurried to the cemetery and saw Jesus standing with the same man who had once lived among the tombs. By then the man was clothed and in his right mind. He had been set free!

Now, here's the application of that biblical passage. You and I may not be running naked in our town's cemetery, but we can still be influenced by demons. If we have a specific difficulty in our lives, if we have a continued weakness, if we have an area of sin we can't get control over, then we may well be under spiritual attack.

Maybe it's a sin that we've confessed again and again, but we keep falling into it, over and over. Maybe it's an area of life over which we feel powerless. We grit our teeth and resolve not to mess up, but we can't gain the victory, no matter how hard we try.

Maybe there's one dark area in our lives—a past wound or a past dabbling in something illicit. It's something we've kept hidden for years, but it still affects us negatively. We just can't seem to get free of this one dark area. Most likely the problem is spiritual oppression. It's not simply a weakness in our lives, not if we've struggled with it for any amount of time.

Take heart—there's hope ahead. I've been in ministry for more than thirty years, and the only people I've ever seen who can't get free from spiritual oppression are those who won't admit they can be spiritually oppressed.

Let's look at two important biblical facts together.

Fact #1: Demons Really Do Exist

I'd never thought much about the reality of demons until I realized I had spiritual oppression in my life. I was a Christian. I loved the Lord. I'd even started ministering. But I was still very much tied to lust and immorality. I will address this specific area of sin later in this book. But I want to tell you about it right up front in this book to help remove the stigma, shame, and fear associated with being spiritually oppressed. As believers we need to be transparent and accountable to each other about our struggles and weaknesses.

Yes, I was responsible for my own sin. But there were other factors in play that were trapping me in my sin.

I'd be standing in front of a church, preaching God's Word. I'd notice a beautiful woman sitting in the second row, and I would try to use willpower to resist lustful thoughts. I tried everything I could think of to block the thoughts.

I did pray about the problem. I would flip through my Bible, hoping an answer would suddenly become clear. I even read a self-help book or two. But try as I might, I couldn't conquer my problem.

Maybe you have a similar problem you can't get rid of. Maybe you, too, are under the power of lust—or your issue may be unforgiveness, bitterness, anger, gluttony, or despair. You want to break free, but no matter what you try, you can't seem to do it.

If this is your experience, your problem could be the result of spiritual oppression.

One of Satan's greatest strategies is to fool people into thinking he doesn't exist. It's also popular to think of Satan and his horde as a bunch of cartoonish images. Satan is only the little red imp with a forked tail and a pitchfork in his hand, sitting on someone's shoulder. He's laughable, surely not anyone to take seriously—if he even exists.

But Scripture teaches that Satan and his demons are very real. Nothing is comical about them, and we need to take their existence seriously.

In Matthew 12:24, Satan is referred to as "the ruler of the demons"—he leads the pack. The word *demon* appears eighty-two times in the New King James Version of the Bible—eighty in some other versions of Scripture. The count is different simply because the word is translated a little differently.

In the Gospels alone the word *demon* is mentioned sixty-one times. Think about that. Sixty-one times Jesus either dealt directly with demons or talked about demons. The word occurs in the Old Testament and throughout the rest of the New Testament, too, but it shows up more often in the Gospels because it was during this time that Jesus lived on earth, and He came "to set the oppressed free" (Luke 4:18 NIV).

He preached the gospel, healed the sick, and cast out demons (Matthew 11:2–5; Mark 1:34–39), which is exactly what He sent His disciples out to do (Matthew 10:5–8).

Scripture indicates that demons are fallen angels. They're disembodied spirits. Before the dawn of time, a mighty battle took place between good and evil. One-third of the angels sided with Satan and fell along with him (Revelation 12:3–9). That's bad news. But the good news relates to simple math. If one-third fell, then two-thirds didn't fall. We're on the winning team, friends.

The really good news is that, ultimately, math isn't the important factor. Scripture is clear that Jesus is greater than Satan and all the hosts of demons combined. Remember that verse I encouraged you to hold fast to? "He [Jesus] who is in you is greater than he who is in the world" (1 John 4:4).

Demons were real in Jesus' day, and they're real for us today too. If we don't believe in demons, then we need to cut out a lot of the Bible and a lot of Jesus' ministry. Some so-called scholars try to do just that. They claim Jesus only pretended to cast demons out of people because the culture of that day believed in demons. According to this school of thought, naturally occurring physical and mental problems were blamed on demon possession. The common treatment for such problems in the premodern superstitions of the first-century Middle East was to cast out the demons. So Jesus went along with that practice out of respect for that particular culture.

That line of thought is a desecration of Scripture. Don't ever get caught up in heresy like that. In centuries past the medical procedure of bloodletting was commonly used in hopes of curing various sicknesses. We know today that bloodletting is extremely harmful, not helpful. If Jesus had come to earth during the Middle Ages, would He have purposely bled people just so He could fit in? Of course not.

Ephesians 6:11–12 and other passages make it clear that a whole host of literal fallen spirits exist and are present "in latter times"

(1 Timothy 4:1). And why would passages in the Gospels differentiate between sicknesses and demon possession if demonic oppression wasn't real? Matthew 9:32–33, for instance, relates the story of a man who was both "mute and demon-possessed."

In his preface to *The Screwtape Letters*, C. S. Lewis wrote,

> There are two equal and opposite errors into which our race can fall about the devils. One is to disbelieve in their existence. The other is to believe, and to feel an excessive and unhealthy interest in them.[1]

My good friend Pastor Jack Hayford, paraphrasing Lewis, says it this way: "There are two groups of people that Satan absolutely loves and gets excited over: the skeptics and the superstitious."[2]

The skeptics are the people who believe demons don't exist or only existed in Jesus' time. Satan loves these people because if he supposedly doesn't exist, then he's not considered much of a threat, right? If you don't believe in Satan, then there's no reason to heed 1 Peter 5:8 and "be sober, be vigilant; because your adversary the devil walks about like a roaring lion, seeking whom he may devour."

The superstitious, on the other hand, tend to see Satan behind every bush. They believe every problem, every sickness, every malady, every sin is caused by a demon. That's also a deception. The Bible is clear that some problems are just that—problems. They weren't caused by a demon but occur within the normal course of life. After Jesus went into the wilderness and fasted for forty days and nights, He was hungry (Luke 4:1–2). His hunger wasn't caused by a demon. It was simply the result of going without food.

Scripture is also clear that our sins, in much the same way, can be caused by our own lusts (James 1:13–14 NASB), our flesh (human nature—Galatians 5:19–21), the "pride of life" (1 John 2:16), and evil hearts (Mark 7:21–22). Not all sins are prompted by demonic influence. We can't say, "The devil made me do it," every time we slip into problems. It may seem like a great way to get us off the hook, but often it's just not true.

Both the skeptics and the superstitious are deceived, and if you fall into one of those camps, then you need to move to the middle camp. We're not skeptics, and we're not superstitious. We don't deny demons, and we don't see them as the root cause of every problem either. We simply need to know and acknowledge they exist and that spiritual oppression can happen to us.

Fact #2: Demons Can Influence and Oppress People, Even Believers

Within some churches today it's popular to teach that a *d* word—*discipleship*—is the only solution for life's problems. By discipleship we mean people should read the Bible, pray, and follow Jesus. And discipleship is a very good thing. The church I lead is very big on discipleship. The Great Commission found in Matthew 28:18–20 makes it clear that we're to make disciples of people from all nations. We're to baptize them and teach them to observe all the things Jesus commanded. That's discipleship.

But notice that within the scope of Jesus' commandments comes another *d* word—*deliverance*. If a person reads the Bible, prays, and follows the teachings of Jesus, that's good. But sometimes we need to be delivered—released from the bondage of spiritual oppression. Jesus came to set us free, and a person can't get free if he doesn't know he can be oppressed.

Much of the church has underestimated the depth and breadth of the freedom that Jesus died to purchase for us. Yes, in Christ we have been freed from the curse of going to hell when we die. This is the ultimate deliverance. And, certainly, we have been freed from sin's yoke of guilt and shame in this life. Yet there are dimensions of freedom that some believers and their pastors have overlooked.

I have a close friend who was saved during the Jesus movement in the 1970s. Back then he was living the hippie lifestyle—experimenting with drugs, hitchhiking around the country, and doing all the things in that scene. Then he got saved. He began to attend a strong Bible-believing church that understood the reality of spiritual warfare. He went to a solid Bible college that understood spiritual warfare. Then he wanted to minister internationally, so he attended a language school where he met some missionaries from another religious background who didn't believe in spiritual warfare. He was shocked. They believed in demons, sort of, but they certainly would never pray for anyone's deliverance. They believed that God would just take care of things if a person kept going to church and doing good things.

My friend asked them outright, "You don't cast demons out of people?"

And they said, "Well, no."

Then he posed this wonderfully pure question: "So you leave them in?"

The Bible explicitly declares two objectives of Jesus' earthly ministry. His mission was "to seek and to save that which was lost" (Luke 19:10), but it was also to "destroy the works of the devil" (1 John 3:8). As a pastor I have a front-row seat to observe such works of the devil and his minions. I've seen them shackle people to unhealthy life habits, patterns of destructive behavior, and cycles of defeat. And, yes, there are physical and mental components to many of these addictions, compulsions, and bondages. But there is a clear and real spiritual component, too, and it definitely doesn't happen to nonbelievers only.

We may be born-again, well acquainted with God's Word, and even called to full-time ministry, but that doesn't mean we're automatically going to walk in all of the freedom Jesus died to provide for us. In fact, achieving and maintaining freedom requires attention, effort, and vigilance.

Jesus purchased our freedom in part so we could enjoy a lifestyle of freedom. Yet if we can experience a lifestyle of freedom, then it's logical to assume we can also go the other way and experience a lifestyle of oppression and even bondage. We can fail to walk in all the freedom that belongs to us. The second half of Galatians 5:1 warns us of this very thing: "Stand fast therefore in the liberty by which Christ has made us free, *and do not be entangled again with a yoke of bondage.*"

Part of our challenge in understanding all this is that we tend to think of demons in terms of what we've seen in Hollywood. We picture a girl's head spinning around. Or a man looks in the mirror and sees another face staring back at him. Some overt demonic manifestations may occur from time to time, but demonic influence in our lives is usually much more subtle.

Another problem in understanding may come from the term "demon-possessed," as found in Matthew 4:24 and Mark 1:32 to describe people Jesus healed. The original Greek word is *daimonizomai*—*daimoni* for "demon" and *zomai,* translated "possessed."[3] In English, to possess something means to own it. But *zomai,* used very infrequently, doesn't really mean ownership. It means to have mastery over or to gain control over. For instance, in Luke 21:19, the root word for *zomai* is used in this verse: "By your patience *possess* your souls."[4] Jesus wasn't saying that we need to own our souls because our souls belong to Him. Rather, He was saying that we need to gain control over our souls.

I realize that the phrase "demon possessed" is really loaded these days and that all sorts of red flags immediately come up when it's mentioned. So maybe it's more helpful to think of demon possession as demons "gaining power or influence over" people. Sometimes the influences come from the outside—tempting them to evil or badgering and shaming them about confessed sin. At other times, demonic influence can come from the inside, actually causing people to act or think in certain ways.

Some scholars insist that Christians cannot be influenced by a demon because the Holy Spirit indwells them. If God is living inside a person, they reason, then how can a demon also reside there—or even gain an entry point to harass that individual? But Scripture teaches that God is omnipresent. If God is everywhere and demons can still exist within God's world, then demons can exist where God also exists within a person's body. And if we define possession in its original sense of gaining control over someone, then it's within scriptural bounds to say that demonic influence can come from inside a believer.

A Christian cannot be owned by a demon. No way. But can a Christian be influenced by a demon or come under the control of a demon, even from within? Certainly.

The Louw and Nida *Greek-English Lexicon* offers additional light on demonic influence: "One cannot speak of a person 'being possessed by a demon.' A more appropriate expression may be 'the person possesses a demon.' In other instances an idiomatic phrase is employed, 'the demon rides the person' or 'the demon commands the person.'"[5]

One of the clearest scriptural examples of demonic influence over a believer is found in 2 Corinthians 12:7, where Paul stated, "Because of the surpassing greatness of the revelations, for this reason, to keep me from exalting myself, there was given me a thorn *in the flesh*, a messenger of Satan to torment me" (NASB). Note how Paul said a "messenger" (*angelos*) of Satan had been sent to be a thorn in his "flesh" (*sarki*). These words suggest that an angel of Satan, also known as a demon, was afflicting his physical body.

The spirit of a born-again believer has been made alive and sealed by the Holy Spirit of God (John 6:63; Ephesians 2:1–5; 1 Peter 3:18). But as Paul made clear elsewhere, believers can either live by the flesh or live by the Holy Spirit. According to Ephesians 4:26–27, whenever we choose to live by the flesh (such as when we give in to anger), we "give place" to the devil, giving him an opportunity to influence us. The Greek word used here is *topos*, which means a place or geographical location—from which he can control us. The word is also sometimes translated as "foothold."[6]

Regardless of how the demonic influence comes—from outside or inside our bodies—we're always called to be diligent. We're never called to get weird or unbalanced where these matters are concerned. We're called to maintain a healthy balance between the extremes, by discerning and responding with authority to strongholds and demonic spirits while helping others recognize and accept their own responsibility for their life choices.

If we want to grow as Christians, both *d* words are involved. We need both deliverance *and* discipleship. Pastor Hayford says, "You can't disciple a demon, and you can't cast out the flesh!"[7] Discipleship and deliverance must walk hand in hand.

Good News Ahead

How does a person come to be influenced demonically?

In John 10:1 Jesus said, "Most assuredly, I say to you, he who does not enter the sheepfold by the door, but climbs up some other way, the same is a thief and a robber." The sheepfold is where the sheep are, the believers. The devil comes to steal, kill, and destroy (v. 10), and he can't get in by the door. So he tries to get in some other way. He'll do it by any means made available to him.

Let's say one night you're upstairs in your bedroom, and you hear your doorbell ring. You go downstairs and peek through the peephole and see a robber there. I mean, this robber is clearly a robber. He has a stocking cap over his face with eyeholes cut in it and everything. He's carrying a sawed-off shotgun, and it's pointed straight at your door. He's carrying an empty sack that he clearly wants to fill once he gets inside. He may even be holding a big sign that blatantly states, "Danger! I'm a robber. I'm going to harm you."

What would you do?

Well, undoubtedly you'd barricade your door. You'd get help. You'd phone the police. You'd run upstairs and get the baseball bat you hide under your bed so you could be prepared for the worst.

What *wouldn't* you do? That's pretty clear, isn't it?

You wouldn't open the door just a crack so you could look at the robber more closely. You wouldn't have a conversation with him so you could learn more of his evil ways. You wouldn't shake his hand while he stood on your doorstep, and you certainly wouldn't invite him inside your house so he could sit in your living room for a while and get comfortable.

Guess what? That's exactly what far too many people do when it comes to the demonic thief outside their doors. Instead of resisting the devil (James 4:7), they crack the door open and inadvertently invite him inside.

Let's say a Christian drinks too much alcohol and becomes drunk. Then, tragically, she climbs into her car, begins driving, and causes an accident, maybe even a death. Does the alcohol own that woman? No, she's still a believer. She's still owned by God. But she was clearly *under the influence of* that alcohol. The alcohol caused her to do something totally out of character. She harmed people. She harmed herself. When she consumed too much alcohol, she opened the door for evil to influence her.

Or let's say a man looks at pornography. He's just opened a door to the enemy, and the enemy will push through the crack to get in. The enemy will not own the man, but he will influence the man. Normally, the man is a good husband and father. But with the enemy influencing him, he may wind up doing something totally out of character that shocks him and everybody around him.

At this point you may be starting to worry, thinking you have a problem with spiritual oppression. If you do, I don't want you to feel guilt or shame about it. I don't want you even to feel fear. The good news is that you can be free from the oppression. Satan will try to make you think that only other people can get free but you can't. He'll suggest that you've sinned too greatly or that you're a weak person. But all of that's a lie. Satan does not have the power to stop you from coming to Jesus.

You may have given evil a stronghold in a certain area, but Jesus always offers a way to be free.

In the pages ahead we're going to look more closely at how to get free and what it means to be free, but let's start here right now with the truths we've examined in this chapter. Yes, demons are real. And yes, they really can influence, control, oppress, and possess people. But here's the great news: Jesus really does set people free!

In Luke 10:17, Jesus sent seventy of His disciples out in the Galilean countryside to minister to people. The disciples came back excited with this report: "Lord, even the demons are subject to us in Your name."

Jesus didn't act surprised. Instead, He offered them this victorious reply: "I saw Satan fall like lightning from heaven. Behold, I give you the authority to trample on serpents and scorpions, and over all the power of the enemy, and nothing shall by any means hurt you" (vv. 18–19).

Jesus was not encouraging His disciples to go out and flaunt a spiritual ability to step on snakes and other poisonous creatures. He was responding to their report about the demons. Through the ministry of Jesus, demons were made obedient, submissive slaves.

Jesus didn't end it there. He said, "Nevertheless do not rejoice in this, that the spirits are subject to you, but rather rejoice because your names are written in heaven" (v. 20). That's always the main focus of any spiritual discussion: Jesus offers freedom and life.

And that's where I'd like to end this chapter—on Jesus. He is always the One we want to lift up in praise. He's always the One who gets the glory.

Would you let me pray for you? God is not bound by time and space or the pages of a book. As I'm writing these words I'm praying for you. I'm praying that if you're feeling unsettled in this area, you would realize freedom is offered to you by Jesus. He always cares for you. He always loves you. His arms are always open wide for you to come home.

Pray this with me:

Lord, You are great. In You there is all power and authority. I need to get free. I'm being oppressed. I'm in bondage, and I want to quit making excuses for it. And I don't want to be afraid of it. Lord, in the name of Jesus Christ, please set me free. Amen.

I remember when I first realized I was in bondage, I was highly concerned. But the more I thought about it and the more I went through God's Word, the more hope I had because I realized I could get free.

Here's a promise from God's Word: "So if the Son sets you free, you are truly free" (John 8:36 NLT). That's great news for us. But it's a process. And we need to close the doors and windows of our house to evil. In the next chapter we'll talk more about how to do just that.

Questions for Contemplation or Group Discussion

1. Demons are real. Scripture says that is true—as true for us today as it was for the people in Bible times. Growing up, what beliefs were you taught regarding the supernatural? Do you have a background that caused you to believe demons are not real? Or were you raised in a culture of superstitions, with not only a belief in demons but also a fear of them? Explain.

2. What are some of the indications that a person might be under the influence of a demon?

3. Have you ever been set free from an evil influence in your life? Was it an immediate healing, or did God take you through a process? Explain.

4. Reread 1 John 4:4. What strong truth from this verse do you always need to keep in mind?

5. Ask God to show you if there's an area in your life where He wants you to be set free.

Chapter Two

THREE BIG
WARNING SIGNS

Do not . . . give place to the devil.

—Ephesians 4:26–27

I was a sickly kid, as they used to say. You name it; I came down with it—coughs and colds, earaches and headaches, runny noses and runny eyes, and sore throats and sore stomachs.

I was also accident-prone. When I was just three years old, I wanted to be just like the NASCAR drivers I saw on TV. But I couldn't drive, so I hopped onto my tricycle instead. I pedaled the front wheel with all my might and rounded a few corners with success but soon toppled over hard. My two front teeth drove through my bottom lip, and I actually needed two surgeries to repair the damage. After that my bottom lip was bigger than other kids'. I hated myself for that. When I went to join the school band, the teacher said, "Boy, you'd be great to play the trombone with those big lips." To this day there's still scar tissue I can feel in that lip.

I grew up, but things didn't change much. Over the years I have broken sixteen different bones. I've had so many accidents I lost count—bizarre accidents too. Bicycle accidents. Motorcycle accidents. Horseback-riding accidents. Bull-riding accidents. I even had a Frisbee golf accident. More than once I've preached with my arm in a sling. Right after I was married, I had a lung collapse and needed emergency surgery. I've even been hit by a car. For many years I believed that having so many accidents and being sick so much was normal.

Then, a while back, I got to thinking. *Maybe it isn't normal to be so hurt all the time—not for me, not for anyone. Maybe something else is going on.*

Something spiritual.

I began to study the Bible specifically with an eye to see how Satan can attack us, and I learned pretty quickly that one of the ways he seeks to harm us is by stealing our health.

Now, I'm certainly not saying that every sickness, disease, or accident is a result of spiritual oppression. But certainly the Bible makes allowances for *some* of our infirmities to be caused by these means. Satan is always looking for open doors of opportunity in our lives. He's seeking not to own us, but to control us and influence us—and to hurt us any way he can.

The apostle Paul exhorted us that we are not to be ignorant of the enemy's devices. As we saw in chapter 1, it's possible for us to "give place" to the enemy (Ephesians 4:27), or as the New International Version translates it, to provide him a "foothold." When we undertake certain activities, the devil is given legal grounds to claim his turf. Paul described this ground further in 2 Corinthians 10:4, where he used the word "strongholds."

The good news is that if the trouble in our lives has a spiritual root, then Jesus can easily deliver us and dig out that spiritual root. His work in our lives makes true freedom possible.

What's Our Responsibility?

Our responsibility is to identify those areas in our lives where footholds and strongholds may have been created, those areas where Satan has been given legal grounds. Identification is the first step in us becoming free. That's followed by confession, prayers for deliverance, and the continued filling of the Holy Spirit, as we'll examine in more depth in later chapters.

So let's start with identification. Let's examine our lives and look for three big warning signs that doors in our lives may have been opened to evil. If any of the following is present in our lives, then spiritual oppression is a possibility.

#1: *Continued Iniquity*

Iniquity means sin. Continued iniquity means willful, habitual sin. And that's a sign that we may have allowed some spiritual snakes to slither into our houses.

The Bible says everyone sins and falls short of the glory of God (Romans 3:23). There are some sins that can easily entangle us (Hebrews 12:1 NIV). Some sins are simply caused by our normal fleshly nature (Galatians 5:17). So I'm not saying that every time we sin it's because a demon influenced us, and I'm not saying that every time we sin we become controlled or influenced by a demon.

Yet if we continually sin, particularly over and over in the same specific area, or if we willfully sin while consciously thumbing our noses at God, then that's a big danger sign that something deeper is going on in our lives, something influenced by evil.

The ongoing sin can be both a cause and an effect. Habitual sin in our lives can open the door to evil influence. But the presence of habitual sin can also be evidence that something evil has already moved in.

Say a woman continually finds herself jealous of others. That jealousy can open a door to the evil one. The woman is allowing distorted and deceptive thoughts into her mind that will influence her. These harmful thoughts are certainly not produced by God. So ask yourself: *Where do these thoughts originate?*

We can be in bondage to habitual sin and not even be aware of it.

One of the best illustrations of this in the Bible is found in John 8. Jesus was teaching in the temple. A woman caught in the act of adultery was brought to Him by the scribes and Pharisees. They wanted Jesus to condemn her—literally to give them grounds to throw rocks at her until she died. Instead, Jesus stooped down and wrote on the ground with His finger as though He didn't hear. We're not exactly sure what Jesus wrote on the ground, but when He was finished, He rose up and uttered these famous words: "He who is without sin among you, let him throw a stone at her first" (v. 7).

One by one, the woman's accusers stormed out. Or maybe they walked out hanging their heads in shame—we're not exactly sure how they left. We do know that later they came back to Jesus to ask Him more questions. The text indicates that some of these had come to believe in Him. Jesus said to these believers, "If you abide in My word, you are My disciples indeed. And you shall know the truth, and the truth shall make you free" (vv. 31–32). In other words, Jesus was saying, "Hey, if you truly want to be free, you can be, but it's not a guarantee. You're going to need to abide in My Word."

The offer of abiding is a great gift to receive, but note the response of the Jewish believers. To me, it's one of the most humorous statements in the Bible: "We are Abraham's descendants, and *have never been in bondage* to anyone" (v. 33).

Really? They'd never been in bondage to anyone?

Had they never read their history? Way back when, they'd been slaves in Egypt under Pharaoh. Then, after they'd entered the promised land and a season of victory was over, they'd fallen into habitual idol worship and iniquity. They'd been conquered by a series of national taskmasters—Chaldeans, Babylonians, Assyrians, and Greeks. And at the exact moment they made this statement to Jesus, they were in political bondage to the Romans.

Look at their statement again: "We are Abraham's descendants, and have never been in bondage to anyone."

Wrong. They'd been in bondage to everyone! Talk about living in denial.

Yet before we're too hard on these believing Jews from Jesus' day, let's take a hard look at ourselves. How easy is it to say something like, "Well, Pastor Robert, I get that you're writing a book about spiritual oppression. Good for you. And, sure, other people may need to be delivered from bondage, but not me. I'm a Christian. I've never been in bondage to anyone."

Really?

What about your thought life? What about pride? What about fear or anxiety? Or what about lust or anger or bitterness or resentment or jealousy or a lack of forgiveness?

You bet that Christians today can be in bondage. In fact, in the very next verse, John 8:34, Jesus made it clear exactly who is in bondage. "Most assuredly, I say to you," Jesus said, "whoever commits sin is a slave of sin."

Note the broadness of that category—*whoever commits sin*. That's a lot of people. We know from other passages that Jesus was talking about habitual, willful sin.[1] But here's the good news, and it comes right in the next two verses: Jesus sets us free! Jesus said to them, "A slave does not abide in the house forever, but a son abides forever. Therefore *if the Son makes you free, you shall be free indeed*" (vv. 35–36).

Jesus was not talking about our salvation here. He was saying that as believers we can either choose to live in bondage to the habitual sins that open us to evil influence, or we can choose to walk in the freedom He has given us, as sons and daughters rather than slaves.

The implication is obvious. Jesus was warning us away from sin. He's continually exposing the darkness, persistently holding out the lamp for our feet and the light for our path (Psalm 119:105). He was encouraging us to run in the paths of His commands, for He sets our hearts free (v. 32 WEB).

Look at John 8:34 again: "Whoever commits sin is a slave of sin."

The Greek word translated "commits" is powerful. It means more than simply participating in something. It has the connotation of pledging to do something, of formulating a plan. It's deliberately making choices we know are wrong. So the verse could be read like this: "Whoever *plans* to sin—and then does it—is in bondage to sin."

The same concept is presented in Romans 6:16. The English Standard Version reads, "Do you not know that if you present yourselves to anyone as obedient slaves, you are slaves of the one whom you obey, either of sin, which leads to death, or of obedience, which leads to righteousness?"

Paul was warning believers of the dangers of willful sin. He was saying, "Look: you're going to serve somebody, and whoever you serve is going to be a master over you. You can choose to be either a slave to sin or a servant of Christ. Who are you going to serve? Who will be the benevolent master?"

I knew a young man once who was having an affair. He'd reasoned the matter through and knew it was wrong, yet he insisted he was trapped in the experience and could not stop. Truth be told, he did not *want* to stop. He confided in me that every time he participated in the illicit activity, he enjoyed the adrenaline rush. He just kept sinning and sinning, willfully and habitually.

One day he took some sexually enhancing drugs, and in the very act of adultery, he had a heart attack and died. Remember, he was a young man with an otherwise healthy heart. I don't tell that story to judge him or to throw stones in his direction. I offer it as a strong warning. The young man was a slave to sin. He'd chosen the master he was going to serve. He'd cracked open a door in his life to the enemy, thinking somehow he could escape the dangerous consequences. He died in his sin.

The prophet Jeremiah recorded powerful words coming from God Himself that describe the audacity of willful, habitual sin:

> "Behold, you trust in lying words that cannot profit. Will you steal, murder, commit adultery, swear falsely, burn incense to Baal, and walk after other gods whom you do not know, and then come and stand before Me in this house which is called by My name, and say, 'We are delivered to do all these abominations'? Has this house, which is called by My name, become a den of thieves in your eyes? Behold, I, even I, have seen it," says the Lord. (Jeremiah 7:8–11)

A modern-day paraphrase of that would be, "So, you're actually going to lie and hate your neighbor and lust in your heart and then come to church and act as if nothing's wrong? That's not freedom! That's slavery!"

Paul warned the Galatians not to use their freedom as an occasion for sin (Galatians 5:13). The instruction is direct and simple: don't make plans to sin. In fact, make plans to run from sin. Don't even dabble in it. Stay as far from sin as you can. May God help us never to open a door to Satan and come under his influence.

Are we doing this?

Are we running from sin?

Are we consciously and deliberately keeping short accounts with God, regularly going to Him and confessing our sins, regularly calling upon the Holy Spirit to give us strength to help us resist temptation and walk in paths of light?

If not, if we are deliberately committing sins in one or more areas of our lives and doing them again and again, then that's a sign that evil may have gotten a foothold in us.

#2: Continued Illness

The second big warning sign to watch out for is continued illness, which I talked a little bit about at the start of this chapter. If we're sick a lot or constantly injuring ourselves, then it can be a sign that a door has been opened to spiritual activity. The enemy has come into our house and brought infirmity with him.

Note that sickness and injuries aren't always the result of demonic influence. There are natural consequences in the world in which we live. Germs exist; and if you breathe in or eat some of the bad ones, you may get sick as a result. Sometimes accidents just happen. You're hiking, you step on a loose rock, and you get hurt, or you're riding a bike, and a car hits you. People get old and die. Cancer strikes both the just and the unjust.

But the Bible is clear that Satan wants to harm us, and sometimes he does this through sickness and injury. If you've experience prolonged or repeated illnesses or have had a lot of accidents, then there may be an open door to evil in your life.

In Luke 13, a woman is brought to Jesus. The Bible points out explicitly that she "had been crippled by a spirit for eighteen years." That's demonic oppression. "She was bent over and could not" raise herself up. Jesus called her to Him and said, "Woman, you are set free from your infirmity." He placed His hands on her, "and immediately she straightened up and praised God" (vv. 11–13 NIV).

The Pharisees got mad at Jesus because this healing took place on a Sabbath. Jesus called them hypocrites. If an ox or donkey needed water on the Sabbath, He said, wouldn't they lead it out of the stall to water? Watch what Jesus said next. "Ought not this woman, being a daughter of Abraham, whom Satan has bound—think of it—for eighteen years, be loosed from this bond on the Sabbath?" (v. 16).

The specific description of the woman is important for us in this context. Jesus referred to her as "a daughter of Abraham." Certainly Abraham had literal, biological children—Isaac and Ishmael and their descendants. Yet I believe that Jesus, who is the same yesterday, today, and forever, was using the phrase in a broader sense.

In Galatians 3:29, Paul used the phrase the same broad way. "If you belong to Christ, then you are Abraham's seed, and heirs according to the promise" (NIV). Jesus would have known that, because God's Word is eternal. The book of Galatians was written in the mind of Christ before the foundations of the world. So the Bible tells us that the true children of Abraham are those who belong to Christ. So that phrase is important because it indicates that this woman was a true disciple of Christ. She was a believer, and yet she had been held in bondage for eighteen years.

Again, please hear me—I'm not saying that every time we get sick it's because of spiritual oppression. But the Bible is clear in this passage and others that sickness sometimes can be caused by "a spirit of infirmity." If you have been sick for a long time, maybe it's the result of an open door in your life. Either you opened the door to evil or someone else opened it for you. The good news is that if the problem is the result of spiritual influence, then the problem can be taken care of.

Acts 10:38 describes how "God anointed Jesus of Nazareth with the Holy Spirit and with power, who went about doing good and *healing all who were oppressed by the devil*, for God was with Him." That remedy is still available to us today. James 5:14–16 lays out the process for us:

> Is anyone among you sick? Let him call for the elders of the church, and let them pray over him, anointing him with oil in the name of the Lord. And the prayer of faith will save the sick, and the Lord will raise him up. And if he has committed sins, he will be forgiven. Confess your trespasses to one another, and pray for one another, that you may be healed. The effective, fervent prayer of a righteous man avails much.

I mentioned I had a lot of sicknesses and accidents while growing up and as an adult—including a Frisbee golf accident. It happened during the summer of 2007, while on family vacation in Colorado. On the very first day we were playing Frisbee golf, and I stepped in a small ravine and fell. I broke my foot and shattered my shoulder. This was no small matter. The accident tore my labrum, the ring of cartilage that surrounds the shoulder joint.

You've heard of people needing surgery for a 10 percent tear. The doctor kindly informed me that I'd torn mine 100 percent—literally 360 degrees, all the way around. My arm was basically detached from my shoulder. If not for skin, my arm would have fallen off. The socket was so damaged that surgeons needed to take bone from another part of my body to rebuild it. I still have the screws and pins in there.

Last spring I was traveling and speaking a lot and started to develop migraine headaches due to the stress—or so I thought. On Easter weekend I preached eight times here at our church in Dallas, then jumped on a plane for Australia to speak at two conferences and two churches. After landing I had a migraine, but I powered through and preached ten times in the first seventy-two hours.

And then I was sick—I mean, really sick. Something was seriously wrong with me, and we didn't know what. My migraine was the worst I'd ever experienced. We found a doctor in Australia who asked me how bad the pain was on a scale of one to ten.

"Twelve," I said.

He ran some tests and gave me some injections and oral medicines in addition to the ones I was already taking for my headaches. But I didn't get any better. In fact, my situation went from bad to worse. I started passing blood and was rushed to an emergency room. Then I passed out.

Pretty soon the Australian doctor discovered that all that treatment and medicines I'd been taking had caused my stomach to bleed. The bleeding was near a major artery. In twenty-four hours I had lost a third of my blood. I spent several days in the hospital. Finally I was cleared to fly, so I flew home for more medical care. It took 120 days for me to fully recover.

The Lord really did a work on me during that time. When I was still in Australia, immediately after I'd gotten out of the hospital, I was taken back to our hotel room in preparation for the flight home. For the first five hours I just slept. Then I got up, and I felt ready to try taking a full bath for the first time in a week.

Debbie was with me through all this, so she helped me into the water, then kissed me and said, "I love you." I said, "I love you too," and she walked out of the bathroom to go check on something. My mind began to churn, and I wondered how my wife could ever love a body like mine. I remembered all the things my scarred and ravaged body had put her through. I found I couldn't stop the thoughts. *I don't love this body,* I said to myself. *I don't even like this body. In fact, I hate this body. I've hated this body ever since I was a kid. I always thought men should be strong, and I was too skinny and weak.*

And just then the Lord said, *Robert, that's your problem. You've hated your body your whole life.*

That's when the spiritual healing started to take place. I began to ask the Lord if there had been an open door in my life for the spiritual snakes to slither through. And God said yes. I'd believed a lie—the lie that accidents are normal for me. I couldn't quite put my mind around that, so I needed to dig deeper; then a memory began to surface.

Once when I was young and in the hospital, I heard a nurse make a dire prediction about my life. She said to my father, "You know, your son is accident-prone. He'll be in emergency rooms the rest of his life."

I had let that dire prediction land in my life like a curse. I'd believed that prediction, even though it wasn't true. Over the years I'd repeated that lie to myself: *I'll be in emergency rooms the rest of my life.* And it had come to pass.

But something else was at play in my life as well. First Corinthians 6:18 describes how a person can sin against his own body. The specific context is fornication, yet the general principle holds true for other sins as well. Looking back, I realized I had sinned against my body. I'd been involved in fornication as a young man. And before I was a believer, I'd been involved with illicit drug use, which would affect how I responded later in life to pain medication.

Debbie can take one Benadryl and sleep for three days. Not me. When I was experiencing all those migraines, I'd need to take large doses of medicine to feel any relief, mostly because that early drug use had given me a high tolerance for pain meds. I was still dealing with the effects of my sin, even so many years later.

As believers, we can forget that our bodies are temples of the Holy Spirit (1 Corinthians 3:16–17; 6:19) and actually begin to hate our own bodies. That's not the right perspective to have. All my life I'd had an open door of not seeing my body as a temple of the Lord. I'd seen it as weak and accident-prone, and I hadn't taken care of it the way I should have. That faulty thought process and my resulting behavior had opened a door for the enemy.

God designed our bodies. He knows how they operate best. I believe that what happened to me in Australia was actually a combination of my own willful sinning by not taking care of myself as an adult, the spiritual oppression from my overt sin as a young man, and the fallout of my believing a lie as a child.

This is the big point I want you to understand: if we have any manner of thinking that's contrary to God's Word, then that's an open door to the devil. The thinking might be how we view sexuality—that our needs will only be met through illicit activity. Or it might be in an area of alcoholism or drug abuse or in an area of insecurity or fear. Any of these can open a door to the enemy.

If we don't like our bodies, then that mind-set can be a stronghold the enemy uses against us. If we don't like our bodies, then that opens us to accidents, to sicknesses, to abuse. Remember in the last chapter when we looked at the demon-possessed man who ran around the tombs night and day? The Bible says that he cut himself. He was hurting his own body. The same sort of thing happens today.

We need to see our bodies as God sees them—as temples of the Holy Spirit. God resides in us. We are not our own. We were bought at a price. Our responsibility is to glorify God in our bodies (1 Corinthians 6:20) and not destroy them. First Corinthians 3:17 contains strong words in this regard: "If anyone defiles the temple of God, God will destroy him."

God has a purpose for you and me. We can't fulfill that purpose unless we take care of our bodies. We need to take care of the temple of the Lord.

#3: Continued Influence

By "continued influence," I'm referring to occult practices. If you or either your parent or grandparent ever participated in occult practices, a door was opened to evil influences, and you still could be feeling the effects of that.

The *occult* is a broad term that describes any activity or product associated with "alternate spirituality" or attempts to access or control the supernatural. I'm talking about astrology, horoscopes, tarot cards, Ouija boards, spells, witchcraft, palm reading, sorcery, séances, fortune-telling, tea-leaf reading, crystal-ball reading, communicating with the dead, spirit guides, ESP, telepathy, auras, trances, black magic, poltergeists, psychics, and more. Don't have anything to do with any of this, even those practices that some people consider harmless fun. They are real and put you in a place to connect with the evil supernatural realm. If there's ever an open door to the enemy, it's occult involvement.

In Mark 7:24–30, a woman whose young daughter had an unclean spirit came to Jesus and fell at His feet. The Bible mentions that "the woman was a Greek, a Syro-Phoenician by birth" (v. 26)—which is important, and I'll explain why in a moment. But let's look at the story first and one of the larger questions, how a demon could ever affect a child.

Jesus and His disciples had traveled to the city of Tyre, where they encountered this worried mother, who said her daughter was possessed by a demon and repeatedly asked Jesus to cast it out. Jesus said to her something that sounded strange. "Let the children be filled first, for it is not good to take the children's bread and throw it to the little dogs" (v. 27).

Dogs? Who was He calling a little dog? That doesn't sound very nice.

The woman answered Him, "Yes, Lord, yet even the little dogs under the table eat from the children's crumbs" (v. 28).

Jesus said to her, "For this saying go your way; the demon has gone out of your daughter" (v. 29).

When the woman arrived home, she found her daughter lying on the bed in a right frame of mind, the demon gone, just as Jesus had said.

Notice that the woman wasn't a Jew, but a mixture of nationalities. Her ancestors had intermarried with people from other countries. Now, there's nothing wrong with interracial marriage today. Race isn't the issue. But intermarriage in those days meant a person of God would make an agreement with a person from a country and religion that didn't worship Jehovah, and Scripture prohibited that sort of mixing. God wanted Israel worshipping only Him, and He knew that one of the big ways His people would be led astray was by marrying someone from a different country who worshipped idols.

The woman was Syro-Phoenician by birth, which meant she was from the part of the Roman province of Syria that had once been the region of Phoenicia. That's key, because Phoenicia is considered by most theologians as the seat of the paganism that entered and plagued Israel for centuries. Guess who else had been born in Phoenicia? Jezebel, one of the most wicked people who ever lived, had married King Ahab of Israel and brought with her the occultic practices of Phoenicia.

Being from Phoenicia, the woman who came to Jesus undoubtedly had a background in the occult, and it was already affecting her young daughter. The woman begged Jesus for deliverance. And it initially sounded as though Jesus were putting her down, referring to her as a dog. That sounds harsh and cruel to our ears today, but if you understand biblical language, you'll see that it really wasn't.

Revelation 22:14–15 says, "Blessed are those who do His commandments, that they may have the right to the tree of life, and may enter through the gates into the city. But outside are dogs and sorcerers and sexually immoral and murderers and idolaters, and whoever loves and practices a lie."

Philippians 3:2 says, "Beware of dogs," in the context of being wary of unbelievers, people who profess to be believers but are actually hostile to the faith.

In the biblical sense *dogs* is just a term that refers to unbelievers. Saved people go to heaven; lost people don't go to heaven. "Dogs" refers to lost people. So what Jesus was saying to the woman was that deliverance is only for the "children," namely, people who already believed Jesus was their Savior. A person couldn't have deliverance unless he or she believed that the Messiah brought that deliverance.

But the woman answered Him with a statement of humility. "Yeah, but even dogs get crumbs." It's a statement that implied she accepted what Jesus said was true. She wanted to be part of the plan of salvation any way she could.

Jesus responded to her humility and said, "Your daughter is free."

How do we apply this teaching today?

First, don't have anything to do with the occult. Don't participate in it yourself, and don't allow your children to participate in it. If you participate in Halloween as a family, don't let your children dress up like devils, ghosts, and witches. If your children play video games, board games, or card games, don't let them play games that involve casting spells or contacting the dark side, even in fun. Don't allow your children to watch movies or read books that feature demons or witches. Don't in any way open them up to the occult. You don't want to provide any open doors for the enemy to influence your children.

Second, take a lesson from that Syro-Phoenician woman's humility. Only the prideful believe that being oppressed can't happen to them. The additional application for us is to humble ourselves and accept the freedom and life that Jesus holds forth.

What Will You Do Today?

Have you been involved with habitual, willful sin? Have you hated your body and opened a door to the evil one? Have you dabbled in the occult, or do you have a family background of dangerous spiritual practices?

Doors may be open.

Spiritual snakes may have invaded your house.

Demonic forces may be influencing or oppressing you.

But don't fear. Remember the promises of Scripture: "He who is in you is greater than he who is in the world" (1 John 4:4) and "If the Son makes you free, you shall be free indeed" (John 8:36).

Let's pray together.

Holy Spirit, we pray that You will draw to Yourself every person who needs freedom today and wants to be set free. We humble ourselves. We confess our sins and renounce them to You. We ask for Your hand of deliverance. We pray that all spiritual oppression would be done away with, that You would remove it from our lives. Fill us now to the full measure of Your Holy Spirit. In Jesus' name, amen.

You're on your way to being truly free.

But there's more ahead. Satan is looking for open doors, and there are more open doors than the ones just described. We need to be aware of the tactics the devil uses to gain access to believers' lives. We'll take a look at some of those in the chapters to come.

Questions for Contemplation or Group Discussion

1. Believers can be in bondage to Satan through sin, through sickness, and through demonic influences we allow into our lives. In this chapter we called these *continued iniquity, continued illness,* and *continued influence.* As you examine these three big warning signs, which might be a problem area in your life or in the life of someone close to you?

2. One area where Satan will steal from us is our health. Have you (or someone you know) ever had a sickness or injury that appeared to be demonically caused? How did you recognize it was demonic? How did you pray for healing? What happened?

3. Read John 8:34–36. What are some sins we might be tempted to call weaknesses instead of bondage? How does our identity as children of God help us walk in freedom from sin?

4. The occult is embraced openly in our culture today. Sometimes it is hard to discern what is occult in nature because it is packaged as humor or drama or mainstream entertainment. How would you help a new believer learn to recognize and avoid the harmful influence of the occult?

5. If you recognize any of these warning signs in your life, what steps will you take today toward becoming free?

Chapter Three

BEWARE THE CHALDEANS

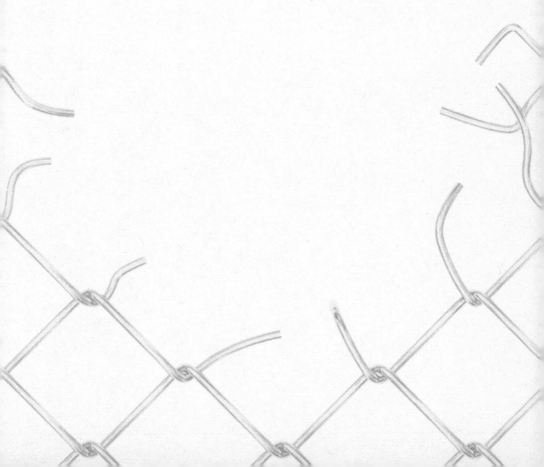

. . . in order that Satan might not outwit us.
For we are not unaware of his schemes.

—2 CORINTHIANS 2:11 NIV

Think about all the dangerous places you've ever been.

You're driving on the freeway in a heavy rainstorm. The road ahead is hard to see, and trucks are splashing up a lot of water. You feel your tires give way around a curve, and your heart skips a beat.

Or maybe you're walking to your car alone at night in a bad section of town. Your pace quickens. You grip your keys tighter. You can feel eyes in the shadows, and you wish you'd brought some pepper spray.

Maybe you're getting ready to skydive or enter a motorcycle race or a boxing ring, and your heart pounds as fear contends with excitement as you prepare to risk life and limb in pursuit of a thrill or a title.

Those situations can all be dangerous, yes. But do you know what one of the most dangerous places is for anyone today—at least someone like me?

A hotel room when I'm all alone.

If we're alone in a hotel room, our normal boundaries of responsibility and accountability seem to shift. We're out of town, and it's easy to feel anonymous even though we aren't really. We can feel catered to and even entitled. We may tell ourselves that we deserve to relax, and maybe that means letting our guard down.

That's a prime opportunity for Satan and his bunch to slither through an open door!

These days Debbie travels with me 98 percent of the time, which I love, so hotel rooms aren't much of an issue for me anymore. But when our kids were younger, I traveled alone a fair bit. Lust has always been a temptation for me, and the easy availability of pornography in hotel rooms was a definite issue. So Debbie and I had an agreement that if I ever felt tempted I would call her instead of turning on the TV.

That's a strategy I'd recommend for any married person, by the way. If you struggle with lust, then let your spouse know about that struggle—and spouses, try to listen without coming unglued. Lust is an addiction, just like a food craving. If your spouse was gone and you ate a box of doughnuts by yourself, it wouldn't mean you don't love him or her. Fight the battle together.

One evening, after a speaking engagement at a church, I found myself alone in a hotel room, and my mind was tempted to go to a dark place. I phoned Debbie, but on that particular evening she wasn't there. Fortunately, a clear voice from the Lord spoke to my heart and said, *"But I'm here. I'm never away from the phone. I never slumber. Talk to Me instead."* The night ended well. Unfortunately I haven't always made the right decisions, and I'll talk about one of those times in a later chapter.

For me, when I am alone, a hotel room with a TV is a spiritually dangerous place, where I'm especially vulnerable to spiritual oppression. For another person it might be a bar or an all-you-can-eat buffet or in front of a computer. Our individual flesh certainly factors into the equation. As James 1:14 says, "Each one is tempted when he is drawn away by his own desires and enticed."

So if we're going to get free—and live free—then we need to know how the devil works and be aware of these dangerous places and situations. As 2 Corinthians 2:11 points out, we do not want Satan to take advantage of us—and that means we need to be aware of his tactics.

We need to know how our enemy works so we can recognize the battles and win the fight.

Know Your Foe

I've heard messages before about how the devil works, and I appreciate any light shined into darkened corners. But a word of caution is needed too. To hear some of these messages, you'd think the speakers were in fifth grade. They trash-talk the devil. They brazenly mock him. They call him names as if he were a playground bully who'd taken away their soccer ball.

Now, I hold no sympathies whatsoever toward the devil. But—and I know this might sound strange—I *respect* him, and I talk about him carefully. Before you slam shut this book in disgust, let me explain that respecting the devil is actually the biblical model. Respect in this case means we have a correct opinion about him as our adversary.

No, we don't like him.

No, we don't admire him.

But we respect him in the sense that a soldier wouldn't go to war armed with a water pistol. A good soldier respects the strength of the army he's fighting against. Respect means we understand that the devil is serious in his approach toward us, and we are not to trifle with him. He is our true foe.

Part of this respect means we don't see the devil as a cartoon character. We don't make flippant jokes about how "the devil made me do it." We don't pretend he doesn't exist. And we don't pretend he doesn't have a strong ability to wreck people's lives.

How does the Bible describe Satan? He is certainly not a man in a red suit with pointy horns, a tail, and a three-pronged pitchfork. He's not the little imp that climbs on our shoulders and whispers, "Hey, Jimmy, steal a cookie." Scripture depicts Satan as a real enemy and makes it clear that we need to be serious in our defenses against his tactics. After all, Jude, the bondservant of Jesus Christ, wrote that even "Michael the archangel, in contending with the devil, when he disputed about the body of Moses, dared not bring against him a reviling accusation, but said, 'The Lord rebuke you'" (v. 9).

The Bible also indicates that Satan has a whole army he uses against us. In my study of Scripture, there appears to be seven categories of satanic underlings, although some scholars interpret the various applicable Bible passages as indicating nine categories. Regardless, it's quite an impressive organization the enemy is running, and it's important for us to see that he's no small-time crook.

- *Thrones*—an indication that Satan has been granted power over certain locations as well as areas of our lives, much like a king seated on a throne (Isaiah 14:9, 13; Colossians 1:16; Revelation 2:13; 13:2).
- *Dominions*—another indication that Satan has been granted certain powers to operate within the unseen world (Colossians 1:16).
- *Rulers*—mentioned in the context of spiritual warfare. Some demons have been granted control over sections of the unseen world (Ephesians 6:12).
- *Authorities*—along with angels and powers, they are subject to Christ's ultimate authority (1 Peter 3:22).
- *Principalities and powers*—part of God's creation that works in invisibility (Ephesians 6:12; Colossians 1:16).
- *Rulers of the darkness*—mentioned in the context of spiritual warfare (Ephesians 6:12).
- *Unclean and evil spirits*—spirit beings who have been granted permission to harass and negatively influence people (Matthew 10:1; 12:43; Luke 7:21; 8:2; Acts 19:12).

To become free of his influence, therefore, we must become aware of what he's like and the strategies he uses. In other words, we need to know our enemy.

Let's look at three biblical descriptions that can help us do that.

#1: Satan Is a Destroyer

The Bible is clear that Satan is an aggressive, venomous snake. John 10:10 says he comes to "steal, and to kill, and to destroy." Whatever good we have in our lives, Satan wants to steal from us. Whatever is true, noble, right, pure, lovely, admirable, excellent, or praiseworthy (Philippians 4:8 NIV), he wants to twist, distort, and ruin. Ultimately he seeks our deaths—sometimes spiritually, meaning he wants us to feel separated from God, and sometimes physically, meaning he actually wants to see our bodies lying in the ground, covered with dirt.

Now, one small clarification: I've had people say something like this to me: "Satan came to me and tempted me to do so and so." I seriously doubt that was the case. The person was undoubtedly tempted, but it probably wasn't Satan who did it.

Many times when the Bible talks about Satan, the descriptions refer actually to the works of Satan and his demons, not just Satan himself. That's because Satan is not omnipresent. He is a limited being and can be in only one location at a time. Only God is omnipresent. He's the only being who can be everywhere at once. Satan leads the demons, and demons are not omnipresent either. But demons can be in more places than Satan because there are many more of them. So they are the ones who usually do the work for him. Scripture does indicate that Satan himself tempted Jesus, of course, but I doubt that the rest of us merit Satan's personal attention. Ultimately it doesn't matter. Satan has an army of demons to do his work for him, and that's what we need to be on guard against.

The book of Habakkuk gives us further insight into the enemy's destructive tactics. Habakkuk is not a book of the Bible we read very often, but it, like all Scripture, can speak profitably to us (2 Timothy 3:16). And a passage from the book of Acts helps illuminate the Habakkuk text.

According to Acts 13, Paul was traveling around on his missionary journeys, spreading the good news of Jesus, when he came to Antioch, a city in the region of Pisidia. There he addressed a large crowd. (Note that there was a different city called Antioch in Syria, which had a large New Testament church. There were two cities with the same name—sort of like Paris, France, and Paris, Texas.)

Apparently there were both spiritually minded Jews and interested Gentiles in this crowd because Paul specifically addressed two groups in his speech: "men of Israel" and "you who fear God" (v. 16). Paul gave them a message about Jesus and ended with a caution that is particularly important to this study. That caution is where he quoted Habakkuk:

Therefore let it be known to you, brethren, that through [Jesus] is preached to you the forgiveness of sins; and by Him everyone who believes is justified from all things from which you could not be justified by the law of Moses. Beware therefore, lest what has been spoken in the prophets come upon you:

"Behold, you despisers,
Marvel and perish!
For I work a work in your days,
A work which you will by no means believe,
Though one were to declare it to you." (vv. 38–41)

Basically Paul was saying to them, "Look: Jesus died on the cross for your sins. He's the Messiah you've been longing for. But you're going to have trouble believing this, because"—and here Paul quoted Habakkuk—"an enemy is trying to blind you."

What is so important about the Habakkuk quote? Taken from Habakkuk 1:5, it warns of blindness toward an incredibly destructive enemy. The following verse names that enemy—the Chaldeans[1]—and describes them:

A bitter and hasty nation
Which marches through the breadth of the earth,
To possess dwelling places that are not theirs. (v. 6)

In Habakkuk's day (the book was written about 605 BC), the Chaldeans were a tribe of people that God was raising up in judgment against the by-then wicked people of Judah. The Chaldeans ruled over most of Babylonia, a territory of about eight thousand square miles—about the size of New Jersey. On today's map Chaldea falls inside Iraq, with its southwestern tip touching Kuwait.

The ancient Chaldeans were known for being an idol-worshipping, highly violent people who marched through the earth intent upon possessing dwelling places that weren't theirs. King Nebuchadnezzar, the famous king of Babylon mentioned in the book of Daniel, was a Chaldean. When he conquered Judah, he stole all the valuables of the land and carried them back to his kingdom. He also stole the next generation of Judah. He brought with him back to Babylon all the fine-featured, intelligent, quick-learning young men of Israel and forced them to study the "language and literature of the Chaldeans" (Daniel 1:3–5).

Later his talons really came out. Nebuchadnezzar commissioned a ninety-foot statue of himself and commanded all the people in his land to worship it. Three young Hebrew men, Shadrach, Meshach, and Abednego (these were their Chaldean names; their Hebrew names were actually Hananiah, Mishael, and Azariah), were thrown into a fiery furnace because they disobeyed Nebuchadnezzar and wouldn't worship the statue.

As recorded in Habakkuk, the Chaldeans were referred to as an actual people. But when Paul quoted Habakkuk, he was actually describing the enemies of God—spiritual entities who, like the Chaldeans, were bent on gaining control over dwelling places that don't belong to them. In other words, they were Satan and his demons.

How do we know this? Because by the time Paul talked about the Chaldeans being a threat to the people in Antioch, there were no more actual Chaldeans around. They had been conquered by Cyrus the Great, king of Persia, in 539 BC. (A prophetic description of the destruction of the Babylonian Empire, which the Chaldeans ruled for a time, is given in Jeremiah 50–51.) After 539 BC, the Chaldeans were never again referred to as a nation or even as an ethnic group.

Obviously Paul wouldn't warn his listeners against a group of people who no longer existed. So who was Paul warning his listeners about?

The name *Chaldean* means "wanderer." The root of the word means "to lay waste or to destroy."[2] The historical Chaldeans conquered lands, robbed people of their money and goods, and stole the next generation—the young future leaders—brainwashing their minds and morals.

The metaphoric Chaldeans of Paul's day—and today—were demons with the same destructive aims and strategies. They want to take control of territories that aren't theirs. They want to steal our minds, money, and morals. And they do it by trying to influence what we put in our minds, what we put in our bodies, and what we give (or don't give) to the Lord. Just like a country of invaders bearing down on an unsuspecting people, they will try to steal our peace and joy. In return, they will leave worry, anxiety, fear, and stress.

But here's the good news: we can take action to combat this. The borders of our land can be sealed tight. The doors and windows of our houses can be locked. The squatters can be evicted and all of our rooms can be filled with the Word of God. All that we value can be kept safe under the lordship of Christ, never to be stolen away.

Let's get very practical for a moment. It's actually possible—and a great practice—to fill our lives and our homes with the Word of God. Psalm 1 encourages us to read the Bible continually to get it into our minds. Write Bible verses on chalkboards and whiteboards in every room. Copy them onto sticky notes and place them on sinks, mirrors, and bureaus. Display plaques, posters, or artwork that features Scripture. Having the Word of God ever before us is one of the most effective means we can find to stop the invaders.

#2: *Satan Is Vicious*

Satan is a destroyer first. He and his bunch are always seeking to control territory that isn't his so he can lay waste to it. And they are also vicious. They never have a good day. They never have a merciful moment. Not one.

Just as the Chaldeans of Habakkuk's day were terrible, dreadful, and fierce, so, too, are the demons of today. Several Scripture passages describe demons as wolves.[3] Can you picture a wolf? A wolf is a predator. It's not kind and cuddly. Neither is a demon—or a person influenced by a demon.

Ezekiel 22:27 says, "Her princes in her midst are like wolves tearing the prey, to shed blood, to destroy people, and to get dishonest gain."

Zephaniah 3:3 says,

> *Her princes in her midst are roaring lions;*
> *Her judges are evening wolves*
> *That leave not a bone till morning.*

In both passages the writers were describing leaders of Israel who were under the influence of demons. And what's most telling in these descriptions is the degree of savagery associated with these princes. They shed blood. They devour and destroy their prey.

Note also how the judges in the Zephaniah passage are described as "evening wolves." Nighttime is a particularly vulnerable time for God's people. Satan loves to oppress God's people when the lights are off. If ever we can't sleep, the best thing we can do is read the Bible and pray.

Several young adults I know have worked at Christian camps, and one told me not long ago that he never allowed the children under his care to tell ghost stories at night. A few of his coworkers mocked him, wondering where the harm was in telling a few scary stories around the campfire. Yet my friend stuck to his ground. He was no coward, but he remembered being a child and being highly afraid at camp whenever ghost stories were told. The stories always seemed to begin innocently enough, but soon they would always morph into tales of the darkly supernatural, of occult activity and the demonic. "Why would we ever associate fear with Christian camping?" my friend asked. I agreed wholeheartedly. Satan loves to prey on our fears, particularly at night when it's easiest.

If you have a habit of watching horror movies or reading scary books (or of letting your kids watch or read them), I encourage you to end this immediately. Don't allow evil to come into your house and fill your family's minds. I understand that some so-called slasher movies are designed to mock fear—they're mostly funny in a dark sort of way. But other movies certainly aren't. They're designed to be exhibitions of gore, violence, demonic activity, and evil. Many of the slasher flicks are also gore-fests. All of them are designed to create an adrenaline rush in us, and it's easy for people to become dependent on that rush and continually want to wallow in that darkness. Nothing good can come from viewing or reading these products.

In Acts 20:29, Paul issued this strong warning: "After my departure savage wolves will come in among you, not sparing the flock." Paul wasn't talking about literal wolves. Again, he was talking about leaders being in bondage to demons. Paul called them wolves—and wolves aren't kind.

Some friends of mine are ranchers in the northwest part of the United States. Lately there's been a real controversy in their area concerning wolves. In decades past, wolves were seen only as predators. They were systematically eradicated until scarcely a wolf could be found in that region. But in modern days there's been a strong movement to reintroduce wolves into certain regions of the States. Some people insist the wolves are necessary to the ecosystem, and they've successfully lobbied the government to allow the wolves back in.

But my rancher friends describe a different reality: wolves are predators and will always be predators. With wolves now reintroduced, the ranchers can't let their children play in their own backyards for fear that they will be mauled. Consistently the ranchers lose valuable cattle and sheep because predators are again on the loose in the area. The ranchers can't go for walks on their own property anymore without carrying loaded rifles.

Another friend of mind participated in a scientific study on wolves. Shortly after I first preached on this subject, he sent me a text:

> The Lord did not teach us about predators to teach animal control or children's fables. Wolves and sheep cannot coexist. When wolves appear most casual and innocent, even interesting to watch, they're actually studying you and sizing up their prey for the attack. The more indifferent they seem, the more serious the danger. They are preparing for the pack attack. The more comfortable they appear, the more deadly they are.

That's a great description of the way demons work. They watch and study people to look for the weak times, the isolated times, the vulnerable times when a person is hurt, frustrated, angry, hungry, lonely, or tired. That's when they attack. And they are never merciful. A demon doesn't say, "Oh, poor Robert. He's had a hard day. I better go easy on him." When a person has a tough time or goes through a tragedy in his life, that's when the hosts of Satan attack most viciously.

The historic Chaldeans lived in marshy regions until they took over Babylon. They were known to be expert archers. When their enemies were trudging through marshes, trying to look where they were stepping, that's when the Chaldeans would shoot them. It's the same way with today's demonic "Chaldeans." When you're trudging through life, that's when they will attack.

How do they attack exactly? In the Bible Satan is described as a murderer and a liar (John 8:44), a confirmed sinner (1 John 3:8), and our adversary (1 Peter 5:8). Satan deceives the nations (Revelation 20:3), and blinds the minds of unbelievers (2 Corinthians 4:4). He snatches the Word of God from unbelievers' hearts (Luke 8:12) and uses men to oppose God's work (Revelation 2:13).

When it comes to Christians, Satan and his demons tempt us to lie (Acts 5:3). They can hinder our work (1 Thessalonians 2:18) and tempt us in the direction of immorality (1 Corinthians 7:5).[4]

Another favorite satanic strategy is to accuse believers. The Bible tells us that Satan does this day and night (Revelation 12:10). He is constantly laying a heavy cloud of shame on us, insisting that we are worthless. He tries to convince us that we've sinned too much for God to forgive us. Or that we were never loved by God in the first place. Or, when we go through trials, that God has abandoned us. Satan spins lies about us, trying to convince us that we are incompetent, unworthy, unacceptable, unlovable, powerless, and disconnected. He always wants us to see ourselves as less than honored heirs of God. And at the same time, he tries to convince us that we have to meet an impossible standard of perfection in order to be loved and accepted.

The Bible also teaches that demons oppose our spiritual growth by spreading false doctrine (1 Timothy 4:1). Everything that comes from God will align with the Bible. If we hear anything from a preacher, speaker, Bible teacher, or friend that is contrary to God's Word, then it's not of the Lord. It's taught by demons. Demonic teaching leads to immoral conduct. It teaches us to be hypocrites, to lie, and to abstain from goodness.

Make no mistake—Satan is vicious. Look at the circumstances surrounding the birth of Moses. Due to the work of Satan, all the Hebrew baby boys under the age of two living in the land of Egypt were thrust through with the sword. The same thing happened in Bethlehem when Jesus was born. Demons respect neither the young nor the old. Satan and his demons are malicious, brutal, ruthless, and cruel.

To combat this, the church acts as a protective sheepfold—guarded, of course, by the Good Shepherd. The people of God act as a buffer between us and the enemy. A sheep that's off to himself, away from the flock, is open to attack. The solution to such isolation is *insulation*.

That's good reason not to remain on the fringes of the church. Particularly if you're going through a difficult time, do not keep yourself away from other Christians. Just nudge your way right into the middle of the flock—*excuse me, excuse me, excuse me*—and get right next to the Shepherd.

#3: Satan Is Cunning

First, Satan is a destroyer. Second, he's vicious. And third, he's cunning. That means he's crafty. He's shrewd. He's deceptive. He seeks opportunities to do his evil work wherever and however he can find them. In Satan's mind, the end always justifies the means.

It's true the historic Chaldeans were vicious fighters, but did you ever wonder how they took over Babylonia in the first place? The first Chaldeans went into the nation not as warriors but as friends. The Babylonian people became used to their presence. They felt comfortable around the Chaldeans. That's when the Chaldeans slowly began to take over. They came in craftily. And then they showed their true colors.

After the Chaldeans rose to prominence, they held all the prominent positions in the land, including priest (to idols) and sorcerer. In Daniel 2:2 the term *Chaldean* is included right alongside references to astrologers and magicians. "Then the king gave the command to call the magicians, the astrologers, the sorcerers, and the Chaldeans to tell the king his dreams. So they came and stood before the king."

Sum up that verse and what does it say? Magicians distract people so they can deceive them. Astrologers try to predict the future. Sorcerers are in contact with the supernatural. The Chaldeans were trying to distract, deceive, and determine the future.

That's exactly what Satan tries to do to us today. He tries to distract us from what's important in life. He deceives us because he's a liar. And he tries to determine our future by pointing us down a path of destruction. Don't listen to him!

Habakkuk 1:15 describes the Chaldeans as fishermen with a hook and net, hoping to catch people for their destruction. There's nothing evil about sport fishing. But consider the principle of effective fishing: it's all about placing a lure in front of the eyes of the prey. That's how Satan acts with us. He never shows us his barbed hook—the dangerous part of his plan. He shows us only what we love—the tasty bait.

That's how Satan acted when he tempted Jesus. Satan showed him bait. After fasting forty days and nights, Jesus was hungry. So Satan offered him bread (Matthew 4:3). There's nothing wrong with bread, but this bread disguised the devil's plans. Satan offered him the easy way out.

And who else but a deceptive mastermind could put a beautiful woman in her bathtub at the exact time King David would walk on his balcony (2 Samuel 11:2–6)? Satan had studied David. Demons watched David's movements, and they knew exactly when he walked on that balcony every night. That's when they put it in Bathsheba's mind to go take a bath. Or perhaps they had studied Bathsheba's movements, and they knew her schedule, so they put it in King David's mind to go take a walk at that exact moment.

Never forget—Satan is cunning. He's smart and deceptive. And he never plays by the rules.

Paul in Ephesians 6:11 encourages us to "put on the whole armor of God, that [we] may be able to stand against the wiles of the devil." The Greek word translated as "wiles" is *methodeia*,[5] from which we get our English word *method*. Use of this word indicates that Satan has plans. He schemes against us.

I mentioned earlier that when a person has a tough time or goes through a tragedy in his life, that's when Satan attacks his hardest. But Satan seldom attacks head-on. At first, he suggests disappointment. Then he slowly turns up the heat. Disappointment leads to depression, then to despair or rage. At each juncture he'll show us options to ease our pain. These options typically look good on the surface. In the end they'll destroy a person.

Daniel 7:25 speaks about one of the devil's cunning tactics. The verse says that Satan shall "persecute the saints of the Most High." Yet the word *persecute* here is not the best translation. The original word literally means "to wear out" or "to harass constantly," from which we get our word *weary*.[6]

Satan will attack us when we're weary. He wants to exhaust us, either through life's busyness or life's hardships. That's when he swoops in for the kill.

Satan just loves it when we're exhausted. I learned this the hard way.

A few years ago I went through one of the busiest times in my life. Debbie and I went to Angola with a film crew on behalf of a mission agency to document the effects of malnutrition and to aid in the care of people there. I came back from the trip physically, mentally, emotionally, and spiritually exhausted but immediately jumped back into my normal, hectic schedule at the church.

A few weeks later I got up for work one morning, showered, put a towel around me, and went to get dressed. I was still wearied, physically and emotionally exhausted. I opened my underwear drawer and only had one pair, so I put them on. For a long time I stood there trying to figure out what I was going to do the next day if I was out of underwear. Then I opened my sock drawer and saw I was out of socks. That nearly did me in. First I needed underwear, and now I needed socks. Socks! Waves of stress flooded over me. Overwhelmed with life's simplest tasks, I sat down in my closet and started crying. I just couldn't function.

We all have four "tanks of fuel" that we draw on every day: an emotional tank, a mental tank, a physical tank, and a spiritual tank. All of my tanks were being drained, and I wasn't filling them up in between intense activities. I remember talking to the Lord about this and saying, "God, I don't think You want me ministering with somewhere between empty and a quarter tank. I need to get my fuel level up around three-quarters of a tank at least."

The Lord spoke to me and said, *Actually I want your tanks to be full—more than full. I don't want you leading when you're on empty or running low. I want you to minister from an overflowing tank. Come to Me. I will give you rest* (Matthew 11:28).

Weariness happens to everyone, which means that rest must be regularly scheduled if we want to avoid making ourselves vulnerable to our cunning enemy. It took me a while to learn this practice, but now I do it consistently. It's early in the calendar year as I write this book, but I already have all my rest days scheduled for the remainder of the year. I use these days to separate myself from my normal activities and to allow Jesus to fill up my tanks.

Words of Hope

I don't want to leave this chapter without offering you big hope for today. We'll talk about solutions more in depth in chapters to come, but I realize it takes time to process this material, and I don't want to leave you without hope right now.

A key verse to remember is 1 Peter 5:8: "Be sober, be vigilant; because your adversary the devil walks about like a roaring lion, seeking whom he may devour." Part of the solution is simply to be sober and vigilant.

Being sober means we stay in control of ourselves through the power of the Holy Spirit. We don't let anything else be in control of us. A person who is drunk is not in control. Ephesians 5:18 exhorts us to "not be drunk with wine . . . but be filled with the Spirit."

Being vigilant means to be watchful. It means we are not afraid of Satan, and we're not unaware of his schemes.

The truth about that "roaring lion" is that Jesus has already pulled all his teeth. Jesus has taken care of evil by the work He did on the cross. We still struggle with the vestiges of evil, yes, but Revelation 5:5 says that "the Lion of the tribe of Judah . . . has prevailed." Jesus Christ has won the victory!

The biggest solution to spiritual oppression always is to stay close to the Shepherd. Undoubtedly you've heard Psalm 23:

> *The LORD is my shepherd;*
> *I shall not want. . . .*
> *Yea, though I walk through the valley of the shadow of death,*
> *I will fear no evil;*
> *For You are with me;*
> *Your rod and Your staff, they comfort me.* (vv. 1, 4)

The passage says that the Shepherd's rod and staff comfort us. Sometimes we get a faulty picture in our minds that the shepherd goes around with his rod hitting sheep. But that's not how it works. A shepherd's rod is used to guide sheep, to gently keep them where they need to be. And it is used for one other purpose—to beat the snot out of the wolf!

That's what the Lord does for us. If you're feeling oppressed by evil, then run to the Shepherd. Run to the Lord!

Let's close this chapter in prayer.

Father God, I pray that we will not be unaware of the devil's schemes. I pray that he will not outwit us—that we will be sober-minded and vigilant and that we will always flee to You. Thank You for Your safety, guidance, and protection. You are Lord of our lives. We love You. In the strong name of Jesus, amen.

You're on your way to being free. But the battle isn't over yet. One of the most common open doors to spiritual oppression is something believers often think doesn't apply to them. But it's actually the biggest demonic trap for Christians as we'll see in the chapter to come.

Questions for Contemplation or Group Discussion

1. What do demons steal from us?
2. How does filling our hearts with the Word of God keep the enemy from stealing from us?
3. Wolves attack prey that is on the fringe of the group. How does being isolated from other Christians make us more vulnerable to attack by the enemy? Do you know anyone who might be isolated? What can you do to invite that person back into connection and relationship?
4. Read 1 Peter 5:8. Practically speaking, what does it mean in your life to be sober and vigilant?
5. In what area(s) of your life is the enemy attacking you (or in what area are you especially vulnerable)? What is God teaching you as you fight this battle?

Chapter Four

BREAKING THE
SNARE OF PRIDE

Pride goes before destruction,
And a haughty spirit before a fall.

—PROVERBS 16:18

G ateway Church, where I serve as lead pastor, is a relatively new church. It's also a large church. The rapid growth has been a tremendous blessing, but sometimes it's also been a cause for stress.

We held our first service on April 23, 2000, Easter morning, with a little less than two hundred people in attendance. The next Sunday our numbers dwindled to sixty-eight—and we counted one pregnant woman as two people. That first sermon must have been a bomb. But by the end of the first year, our attendance was regularly about two hundred people. I felt good about that. The church seemed to be growing steadily and manageably, the way it should. The pace felt brisk, but I felt on top of things.

By the second year, we'd tripled our weekly attendance to six hundred people. That amount of growth felt exciting but nerve-racking at the same time.

By the end of the third year, we had tripled again to eighteen hundred people.

And by the end of the fourth year, we had doubled that—thirty-six hundred people.

By then I was leading by scramble management. It felt as if I were holding on to a speeding train with one hand and was completely horizontal, like a flag flying off the end of that train. I wasn't holding on with two hands, not even holding on with one hand. I had two slim fingers holding on to the end of that train. And what truly frightened me was that I was supposed to be the engineer.

Then Gateway's attendance absolutely exploded.

At the time I'm writing this book, we have about twenty-seven thousand people attending Gateway each week, with more than fifty thousand in attendance Easter Sunday. We currently hold twenty-four weekend services at five locations across the Dallas–Fort Worth Metroplex. We see about five thousand people a year profess faith in Christ for the first time.

The numbers are staggering to me—and I don't mention them to brag about anything I've done. I mention those numbers for the exact opposite reason, in fact. There is absolutely no way I could have ever produced any of what has happened.

By contrast, here's what it looks like when Robert Morris thinks he's in control. Once, during Gateway's fourth year, I took a quick vacation in the mountains of Colorado. For months I'd been feeling nervous and anxiety-ridden and exhausted. The pace at the church was killing me, and I desperately needed a rest.

There, looking out on the grandeur of the Rocky Mountains, I opened my Bible to the book of Exodus, and I poured out my heart in prayer: *Lord, now I know why Moses argued with You as much as he did. Moses was a reluctant leader, and so am I. I don't know if I can do this. I'm always so stressed-out. This church is too large. It's unmanageable. It's gotten too big for me, and I don't think I can go on.*

And God impressed upon my heart in a clear, quiet voice, *You're right, Robert. Gateway Church has gotten too big for you. In fact, everything I've ever called you to do is too big for you. This church growth hasn't happened because of anything you've done. It's all happened because of Me. Now trust Me in this. Go get some more people to help you lead, and then hang on for the ride.*

Do you see the root problem in my initial prayer? It wasn't that I was stressed—that was only a symptom. The root problem was I thought I should be able to handle Gateway Church on my own. That was an indication of my pride. It was me nodding my head toward self-sufficiency.

Pride occurs anytime we say or think, "Thanks, God, but I got this." And it can easily become a demonic trap.

You see, the only reason I'm allowed to preach God's Word is God's grace. The only reason I'm allowed to minister to others is God's grace. The only reason I'm allowed to introduce a person to salvation in Jesus Christ is God's grace. The only reason I can live or move or breathe is because of God's grace.

Each day God extends a gracious invitation to me. He wants to carry me by His strength, and so He invites me to be on my knees every morning, saying,

God, the events of this day are beyond me. The sun will only rise because You say it will. By Your power and mercy this day I will listen for Your voice and do Your will. I will serve You wholeheartedly with the power You give me, and only with that power. This day is of You and for You and from You. I am Your servant. You lead; I'll follow. Amen.

Yours is a similar invitation.

God has called you to a ministry that's beyond your own strength. You may not think that you have a ministry beyond yourself, but you do.

It might be as straightforward as going to work each morning to a job where you're called to be salt and light to a world that desperately needs Jesus. Or it may involve caring for your children so that the next generation rises up to praise the name of God. Maybe you're in a marriage that's difficult, and you need to remind yourself daily to love the person you're yoked to because God commanded you to love. Or maybe you're caring for your elderly parents, and it burdens your heart to see them struggle with the brutalities of aging. Or maybe God is calling you to lead a small group at your church or speak the Word of God each week to a Sunday school class of fifth graders or work in the nursery in the strategic ministry of caring for the church's very young.

Whatever your ministry is, *you can't do it in your own strength.* That thought is both staggering and freeing. Staggering because when you grasp the totality of what God has called you to, then the dream emerges as bigger and deeper and wider than you first imagined. Freeing because if your calling is truly of the Lord, then you can have the full assurance that Jesus is in control—and wherever God guides, God provides.

Being totally dependent on God isn't an easy truth to grasp. The point is never that we see ourselves as worthless, incompetent, or inept. We are paradoxically called to be both powerless people and capable people at the same time. Powerless because it is always God who acts in us to work all things "according to the counsel of His will" (Ephesians 1:11). Capable because we are always called to see our identity in light of what God says about us. We are children of the king (2 Corinthians 6:18). We are a chosen people and a royal priesthood (1 Peter 2:9 NIV). We are wholly and dearly loved heirs of God (Romans 8:17). And as Philippians 4:13 reminds us, we "can do all things through Christ who strengthens" us.

The apostle Paul showed confidence in who God had called him to be and what He had called him to do when he wrote about himself: *"Imitate me,* just as I also imitate Christ" (1 Corinthians 11:1).

Are you dependent on God for everything? Are you both capable and powerless at the same time? If not, that's a root of pride—and it's a big problem.

Whenever I talk about pride, I encounter people who insist they're not proud. But that's a dangerously prideful thought in and of itself. In fact, the number-one open door to spiritual oppression that I've seen over the years in believers has come from this area. Pride is a foothold the devil loves. He loves it because it's so prevalent in people's hearts. And he loves it because it's so sneaky and difficult to detect.

Let's look at three ways pride can show up in our lives and what can be done if it does.

#1: *Trusting in Our Own Strength*

Do you consider yourself a strong person or a weak person? Wait. Don't answer the question too quickly, because the correct answer may surprise you.

The Bible says we are only strong when we are weak (2 Corinthians 12:10). We are strong because of God's power moving within us (Philippians 2:13). God invites us to "be strong in the Lord and in the power of His might" (Ephesians 6:10). But He never expects us to depend on our own strength or to go it without Him. When we try to do that, that's when we fool ourselves and open the door to oppression.

You know who thought he was a strong person apart from the Lord? Peter.

And the Lord showed him otherwise.

At the Last Supper Jesus prayed over the cup and the bread and distributed the food to His disciples. Then a short fight broke out among the Twelve about who should be considered the greatest. Jesus resolved the squabble, and then He turned to Simon Peter and spoke this strange line: "Simon, Simon! Indeed, Satan has asked for you, that he may sift you as wheat. But I have prayed for you, that your faith should not fail; and when you have returned to Me, strengthen your brethren" (Luke 22:31–32).

This amazing passage of Scripture contains a warning we often overlook.

Jesus predicted that Peter would fall away, and we know that Peter understood what Jesus was saying because in the very next verse he tried to dispute it: "Lord, I am ready to go with You, both to prison and to death" (v. 33). Then came Jesus' famous forecast. "I tell you, Peter, the rooster shall not crow this day before you will deny three times that you know Me" (v. 34).

But let's go back and examine that powerful warning in verses 31–32—the promise we often overlook. Note how Jesus said to His disciple Peter, an open follower of Christ, that Satan had asked to sift him.

The Greek word translated "asked" here is stronger than our English word. It means to ask for something with success—to both ask for and receive it. So really the verse could be translated this way: "Simon, Satan *has asked and received permission* to sift you like wheat."

The New American Standard Bible translates that phrase with even more force: "Satan has demanded permission." He has demanded permission only because he has a right. Jesus was warning Peter to watch out because Peter had left a door in his life open to spiritual oppression—Satan has a right to go through open doors.

We have an even clearer picture in a conversation recorded in two of the other synoptic gospels, Matthew and Mark. Jesus said to His disciples,

> "All of you will be made to stumble because of Me this night, for it is written:

> 'I will strike the Shepherd,
> And the sheep will be scattered.'" (Mark 14:27)

Right away Peter spoke up. "Even if all are made to stumble, yet I will not be" (v. 29).

You can almost hear the vehemence in Peter's voice. The disdain. The arrogance. "Look, Jesus," Peter was saying, "all these other weaklings might stumble. But I won't." Then Jesus made His prediction about Peter denying Him three times.

I think Jesus was saying to Peter, "What part of the word *all* don't you understand? *All* of you are going to deny Me. All! There's a scripture in the Old Testament that says you will."

But Peter didn't get it. "No," he said in effect. "The Bible is wrong."

That's pride. He thought he was strong enough to stand.

That wasn't the first time Peter struggled with pride. Back in Matthew 16:21–23 another conversation between Jesus and Peter was recorded:

From that time Jesus began to show to His disciples that He must go to Jerusalem, and suffer many things from the elders and chief priests and scribes, and be killed, and be raised the third day. Then Peter took Him aside and began to rebuke Him, saying, "Far be it from You, Lord; this shall not happen to You!" But He turned and said to Peter, "Get behind Me, Satan! You are an offense to Me, for you are not mindful of the things of God, but the things of men."

Wow, Peter! A person needs to feel awfully good about himself to rebuke Jesus. Note how Jesus didn't even use Peter's name in response. He looked right at His disciple and addressed Satan. Whether Satan was *in* Peter or *on* him or *around* him or *influencing* him is unclear from the text. But we do know for sure that Jesus looked right at Peter and said, "Get behind Me, Satan." Peter was trusting in his own strength. He had opened the door for Satan to influence his thinking—and ultimately the words that came out of his mouth.

Later, in the Garden of Gethsemane, when the soldiers, along with the "officers from the chief priests and Pharisees" (John 18:3), came to arrest Jesus, one of Jesus' disciples tried to take on the whole garrison.[1] Guess who that was? Big, tough, strong Peter, of course (v. 10). According to the various gospel accounts, the officers came with a "great multitude" (Mark 14:43) as well as a "detachment of troops . . . with lanterns, torches, and weapons" (John 18:3). And Peter attempted to fight them with one sword. That's trusting in your own strength. Peter didn't get very far, but he did succeed in cutting off the ear of the high priest's servant.

Because of Peter's pride Jesus had said to him, in effect, "Satan has a right to influence you. You've opened a door to him because of your pride, and now he will influence you, and you will deny Me." That's exactly what happened later on the night Jesus was arrested. Peter was outside the high priest's house, in the courtyard. There, he warmed his hands over a fire. A servant girl took a good look at him and insisted that Peter was a disciple of Christ. Peter started cursing and swearing, saying, "I don't know Him." He did that three times, just as Jesus had said, before hearing the rooster crow (Luke 22:54–62).

The pattern of insistence and denial isn't that uncommon among Christians. Many mature believers fall into this trap, even today. They've walked with the Lord a long time, and then they begin to trust in their own strength. They insist that they can accomplish something or resist temptation on their own or that they can get through a difficult patch if they isolate themselves from other believers.

First Corinthians 10:12 lays out a strong warning for all of us: "Therefore let him who thinks he stands take heed lest he fall."

The straightforward solution to the problem of pride, of trusting in our own strength, is to depend on the Lord always.

#2: *Trusting in Our Own Righteousness*

"By grace you have been saved, through faith . . . not by works" (NIV). Right?

Ephesians 2:8–9 is a passage we love to rattle off anytime someone questions us about trusting in our own righteousness. Of course we don't trust in our own righteousness. We trust in God's grace.

Or do we?

Trusting in our own righteousness is a trap that more of us fall into than you may think. Remember the story of Job? The condensed version is that Satan and God have a great discussion in heaven—some would call it a contest—to see what would happen if a particularly righteous man down on earth had everything he valued systematically taken away from him.

In Job 1:6–7, Satan comes to present himself to God, and God asks, "From where do you come?"

"From going to and fro on the earth," Satan answers, "and from walking back and forth on it." This is right in line with what we know of Satan, that he goes about like a roaring lion seeking whom he may devour.

The rest of the conversation goes like this:

Then the LORD said to Satan, "Have you considered My servant Job, that there is none like him on the earth, a blameless and upright man, one who fears God and shuns evil?"

So Satan answered the LORD and said, "Does Job fear God for nothing? Have You not made a hedge around him, around his household, and around all that he has on every side? You have blessed the work of his hands, and his possessions have increased in the land. But now, stretch out Your hand and touch all that he has, and he will surely curse You to Your face!"

And the LORD said to Satan, "Behold, all that he has is in your power; only do not lay a hand on his person."

So Satan went out from the presence of the LORD. (vv. 8–12)

Basically, God gives Satan permission to oppress Job. This is a problematic idea for some people. But the passage is not difficult to understand when we read the rest of the book.

Later, when Job's life has been wrecked, three of his friends show up and try to comfort him. (You don't want friends like these, by the way). "Look, Job," they keep saying to him, in essence, "are you sure there's not an open door in your life—something the enemy's been able to use against you?" And they rattle off a list of wrongdoings Job has potentially done. But Job says, "Nope, nope, nope. I haven't done any of those wrong things you've listed."

Then, in chapter 32, a young man named Elihu speaks. He's been sitting near the friends the whole time, just listening, but now he basically says, "I didn't say anything all this time because I figured all you guys are old dudes and eventually you'd get the right answer because you're so wise. But none of you have figured it out yet, so I'm going to tell you what the problem is here." Elihu spends a while longer setting up his case; then he hits Job with the clincher in Job 33:8–9:

"Surely you have spoken in my hearing,
And I have heard the sound of your words, saying,
'I am pure, without transgression;
I am innocent, and there is no iniquity in me.'"

Did you catch it? That's the sin of Job's life revealed.

Job believed he was righteous because of the lifestyle he led, not because of the righteous Person he knew.

For thirty-one chapters of the Bible, Job has basically been saying, "Hey, compare me to anybody, and you'll see I'm a good guy. I'm righteous." But Job wasn't righteous—not at the core. He led an upright life, sure. But he was only righteous because of God, and that's whom he failed to give credit to. Job's sin had opened the door for Satan to oppress him, so God granted permission to Satan to go to work.

Believers can so easily fall into the same trap. We think, *Oh, I haven't done this, and I haven't done that, so God must think I'm swell.* We fall into pride because we think that our righteousness comes from us and not from God. But we are not righteous because of what we do. We are righteous by the blood of Jesus Christ alone! Whenever we begin to believe otherwise, that's pride.

God's answer to Job comes at the end of the book of Job. God exposes the man's sin of pride by comparing his finite works and understanding to the infinite works and understanding of God. God asks,

"Where were you when I laid the foundations of the earth?
Tell Me, if you have understanding.
Who determined its measurements?
Surely you know!" (38:4–5)

You can almost hear the divine sarcasm in God's voice as He continues—for almost seventy verses! "Have you ever told the sun when to come up?" (I'm paraphrasing here.) "Does lightning come to your throne and ask where to strike? Do you go hunting for lions and tell eagles how to fly?" (Job 38:12, 25, 39; 39:27).

God ends with this telling statement to Job: "Would you condemn Me that you may be justified?" (Job 40:8).

And to his credit, Job hears these words and repents.

If only more Christians would do the same!

Many mature believers are righteous when it comes to their living, yes, and righteous living is good. Acting the opposite way certainly isn't the solution; unrighteous living only hurts us and opens the door to the demonic. But righteous living does not make us righteous. Only the blood of Jesus Christ does.

A man came to me for counseling once and spent the bulk of our time listing the various troubles he was experiencing. He insisted the troubles were all due to what other people had done wrong. He capped our session by saying, "I've always done the right thing."

I flinched when I heard that and thought, *No, you haven't always done the right thing. Nobody has always done the right thing.*

He was trusting his own righteousness. And that's pride.

The straightforward solution to this pride problem? Always keep in mind that our righteousness comes from God.

#3: *Trusting in Our Own Wisdom*

Debbie and I once counseled a couple who were clearly going in the wrong direction. Near the start of the meeting the problem became evident. I pointed out to the husband a few scriptures with little response from him. After that I stayed fairly quiet throughout the rest of our time together. When we were finished and got in the car, Debbie pursed her lips together. "Hmm," she said, "I thought you would say a little more than you did. What happened in there?"

"The husband is not going to listen no matter how hard we try,"

I said. "I could tell that about him almost immediately. He thinks he's smarter than his wife and wiser than both of us put together, and he had decided early on that he wasn't going to listen to biblical counsel."

"So what's going to happen?" Debbie asked.

"God's going to send the enemy to oppress him," I said. "Hopefully then the husband will repent."

How did I know this?

There's a powerful biblical story found in 1 Kings 22. Ahab was the king of Israel, and he was having a rough go of it. To begin with, he had married extremely poorly. His wife's name was Jezebel, and as we saw in the previous chapter, she was one of the most wicked queens Israel had ever known. Ahab's other big concern was that the city of Ramoth Gilead, which used to belong to Israel, had been taken by Syria. Ahab wanted the city back, but the king of Syria was a bit too powerful for Ahab to attack all by himself. So he found himself in a quandary.

King Ahab met with Jehoshaphat, the king of Judah, who recommended asking a prophet to call on God for advice. So Ahab called the four hundred prophets on his payroll and asked them if they should attack Ramoth Gilead. All four hundred of them said, "Yes, go! God will be with you."

But Jehoshaphat wasn't convinced. "You got any other prophets?" he asked.

"Yeah, I've got one other," Ahab said, or words to that effect. "His name is Micaiah, and he's a true prophet of the Lord. But I hate him because he never prophesies anything good about me. A couple of years ago I put him in prison."

I love the next section of this story, which I'll quote directly from Scripture:

> Then [Micaiah] came to the king; and the king said to him, "Micaiah, shall we go to war against Ramoth Gilead, or shall we refrain?"

And he answered him, "Go and prosper, for the Lord will deliver it into the hand of the king!"

So the king said to him, "How many times shall I make you swear that you tell me nothing but the truth in the name of the Lord?"

Then he said, "I saw all Israel scattered on the mountains, as sheep that have no shepherd. And the Lord said, 'These have no master. Let each return to his house in peace.'"

And the king of Israel said to Jehoshaphat, "Did I not tell you he would not prophesy good concerning me, but evil?" (1 Kings 22:15–18)

Micaiah initially came to Ahab reluctantly. His attitude was, *Well, whatever I say, you're not going to do it anyway, so I may as well tell you whatever you want to hear.* But Ahab pressed him for the real answer, so Micaiah gave it to him. "Don't attack the city. You're going to fail."

Then we come to this telling portion of the story:

Then Micaiah said, "Therefore hear the word of the Lord: I saw the Lord sitting on His throne, and all the host of heaven standing by, on His right hand and on His left. And the Lord said, 'Who will persuade Ahab to go up, that he may fall at Ramoth Gilead?' So one spoke in this manner, and another spoke in that manner. Then a spirit came forward and stood before the Lord, and said, 'I will persuade him.' The Lord said to him, 'In what way?' So he said, 'I will go out and be a lying spirit in the mouth of all his prophets.' And the Lord said, 'You shall persuade him, and also prevail. Go out and do so.' Therefore look! The Lord has put a lying spirit in the mouth of all these prophets of yours, and the Lord has declared disaster against you." (vv. 19–23)

The phrase "all the host of heaven" usually refers to angels, but the phrase makes allowance for fallen angels being present near God's throne too. Notice in this passage that they're standing both on the Lord's right hand and on his left, just as in the judgment of the "sheep and the goats" (believers and nonbelievers) described in Matthew 25:31–46.

Hold both the sheep and the goats and the story of Ahab and Micaiah in mind for a moment, and let me show you another scripture that further defines the host of heaven.

Second Kings 21:1–17 tells the story of Manasseh, who was twelve years old when he became king over Israel and reigned fifty-five years in Jerusalem. Manasseh was a horrible king. He led the nation in idol worship. He practiced soothsaying, used witchcraft, and consulted spiritists and mediums. He even burned his son alive in an act of idolatry. And according to verse 5, "he built altars for all the host of heaven in the two courts of the house of the LORD."

Manasseh wasn't building altars for God here. He was building altars to idols. He worshipped angelic beings. They may or may not have been fallen angels—either way, building altars for all the host of heaven was clearly deemed wrong.

That's important. Remember, we just read in Job where Satan stood in front of the throne of God, and God gave Satan permission to do something. Now look back to the description of Micaiah's vision in 1 Kings 22:20–23. This passage shows the Lord sitting on His throne, a lying spirit talking to Him, and God giving the spirit orders. Note who is always in control. There is not a battle in heaven between God and the devil. The devil is a created being. God is the Creator. God is always in charge, and He will sometimes use the enemy to fulfill His own purposes. Whenever we sin, we open a door to the enemy, and God may give permission for the enemy to oppress us the same way He allowed Simon Peter to be sifted like wheat.

Why would God ever do that? Mark this carefully—it's always for our own good. God is a good Father, and He only disciplines us out of love (Hebrews 12:6 NIV). Do good parents ever discipline their children? Absolutely. Good parents discipline their children because the parents don't want the children going the wrong way. And one way our heavenly Father disciplines us is by letting us get tripped up in our own pride and humbled.

At Gateway, we have both Saturday evening and Sunday morning services, and sometimes the message will be recorded on Saturday evening to be replayed the next morning. I noticed that many of the leaders for these evening services were saying the word "tonight" a lot, which didn't translate well on the video for our morning attendees. So I focused hard and trained myself to say only "today" in those messages. Then I made a big deal to our leadership team about doing the same.

Guess what happened the very next time I got up to talk on a Saturday?

I said "tonight." Several times! And I was humbled.

Proverbs 16:18 is one of the most misquoted verses in the Bible. Usually we hear this verse quoted as "Pride goes before a fall." But look carefully at what the verse actually says:

> *Pride goes before destruction,*
> *And a haughty spirit before a fall.*

Pride does not go before a fall. Pride goes before destruction. Look at the verse again. What goes before a fall is a haughty spirit. But pride goes before destruction. When we have pride in our lives, we will be destroyed—or at the very least, humbled. And one way this can happen is for God in His grace to send the enemy so we go into bondage. If, in bondage, we then humble ourselves and cry out to God, "God, set me free!" He then will set us free.

Or think of it this way. Dabbling in sin is like strolling in front of an oncoming bus. God sees the danger we're in and forcefully pushes us out of the way. We might fall down on the pavement and get scratched up in the process. But the forceful push is actually a push done out of love. Being pushed out of the way prevents us from being destroyed by the oncoming bus.

How does this relate to the danger of trusting in our own wisdom? James 3:14–15 describes it clearly: "But if you have bitter envy and self-seeking in your hearts, do not boast and lie against the truth. This wisdom does not descend from above, but is earthly, sensual, demonic."

If we are dabbling in sin, in other words, chances are good that our conscience or the people around us are warning us that we are in danger. But we're not listening. We think we're smart enough to somehow escape trouble. When that happens, James says, we're listening to the voice of demonic wisdom. We falsely believe that no one can correct us because we somehow have a corner on truth. We think we're either smarter than other people or have more experience or that somehow we've studied harder or thought through an issue more thoroughly. Pride is working overtime in our lives. The door is hanging wide open, and the snake is slithering in.

So would God ever grant permission for Satan to oppress a believer? Absolutely.

We just saw it with Peter.

We just saw it with Job.

We just saw it with Ahab—a man who wasn't following God but knew God's truth nonetheless.

Now think about this: Peter and Job both experienced Satan's oppression, but they repented of their pride. What was the result? Peter became one of the preeminent apostles in the New Testament church. Job had everything Satan had destroyed restored to him—and doubled.

But Ahab?

Ahab didn't repent. He went into battle against Ramoth Gilead anyway, and he was killed. That was no coincidence either. Ahab disguised himself and went into the battle—dressed in ordinary armor instead of the king's robes. But the Bible says a certain man drew his bow at random and shot an arrow that found its way into the joint of Ahab's armor (1 Kings 22:34, 37–38).

Ahab refused to be shoved out of the way of the oncoming bus, so the bus ran over him. God allowed that arrow to destroy Ahab.

The straightforward solution to this third pride problem? We must always trust in God's wisdom alone, and not in any wisdom that doesn't come from God or isn't in alignment with His Word.

Hope for Today

Maybe you read this chapter, and now you're feeling overwhelmed. It feels as though you have a lot of work to do in your spiritual journey. Perhaps you believe you need to get yourself cleaned up first so that God will accept you.

You have pride in your life, yes, and that needs to go. You can't rely on your own wisdom, so you need to seek out biblical wisdom. You're standing in front of an oncoming bus, and you need to get out of the way quickly.

Are you feeling tired already?

But hang on—let me emphasize the work of God in this situation. God always loves us, and the real work of life change always comes from God. Yes, He works with our consent. And yes, there are some things we need to do. We need to repent of our pride and other sins. We need to obey God's commandments and His voice. We need to consent to His leadership in our lives. But the heavy scrubbing of making us clean always comes as a work of God.

I remember when Debbie gave birth to our son, Josh, and I held him right after he was born. The nurse said, "Here, give him over. Let's clean him up first, Dad."

But I didn't hand my son over. (Not right away, anyway.) I didn't care if Josh was cleaned up or not. I just wanted to hold him.

That's the way God feels about us. God holds us when we're bloody and gooey and covered in afterbirth. He sees our sins and our spots and blemishes and loves us in spite of the mess. We don't need to get ourselves cleaned up before we approach God. God always welcomes us with open arms.

Will you pray with me right now?

Holy Spirit, I pray that You will draw every person to Your side who is struggling with pride. Help us to identify pride in our lives and then repent of that pride. We rely on Your strength, not ours, to cleanse us of this pride. We rely on Your righteousness, not ours. We rely on Your wisdom, not ours. Thank You for always loving us and caring for us. Amen.

That's what is necessary to break the snare of pride. God forgives us and works in our lives to make us free. That's really good news.

The bad news is that pride is only one snare that can entangle us. In the chapters ahead we'll look at other doors believers leave open that let in the enemy and, therefore, rob us of joy and leave us defeated.

Questions for Contemplation or Group Discussion

1. Pride means trusting in your own strength, your own righteousness, or your own wisdom. Give some practical examples of how you've seen any of this in your own life or the life of someone you know well.
2. What does it mean to be dependent on God for everything?
3. The chapter says, "Trusting in our own righteousness is a trap that more of us fall into than you may think." What does this mean? Have you ever seen examples of this in your own life?
4. Why is it difficult to remember that God is in control when we are in the middle of a battle?
5. The chapter says, "The real work of life change always comes from God." Explain how this works and what our responsibility is—and isn't—in the midst of that.

Chapter Five

BREAKING THE SNARE
OF BITTERNESS

*Pursue peace with all people, and holiness, . . . lest
any root of bitterness springing up cause trouble.*

—HEBREWS 12:14–15

I was saved at age nineteen after going through some rough years as a teenager. Not long before that, Debbie and I had gotten married, and life took off for us like a jet from a runway. I began working for an evangelist, and soon I was preaching regularly (and confidently) to thousands of people in large churches and stadiums.

Right around that time Debbie and I experienced one of our first big marriage "bumps." We had experienced a few problems before, but those had been my fault. In this case, however, Debbie was most definitely to blame. At least that's how I saw it.

Simply put: Debbie was abandoning me. That was the faulty narrative I told myself, and with that troublesome thought swirling around in my mind, a second problem, a bigger problem, began to grow: feelings of resentment toward my wife. I acted sullen and snappy and edgy. I can remember attending one party in particular, where I felt as if Debbie had abandoned me. I was so upset, I became angry.

"Why'd you leave me alone with all those people tonight?" I hissed at my new bride. "You always do that, and it needs to stop!"

"What's the problem, Robert?" she asked. "All I did was walk across the room."

It took some time for me to open up and realize what was really bothering me. When I dug down deeper, I admitted that I was afraid of what other people thought about me. Sure, I could speak to thousands of people from a pulpit, but I couldn't speak to a handful of people when I was alone with them in a room. I was worried they would meet the real me, the me without a prepared message in front of him, the me who, on the outside, looked like a poised leader but, on the inside, was quaking in his boots. They were sure to hear how ignorant I was. How new a Christian I was. How little I knew my Bible. How I had no business preaching God's Word. How ashamed I was of so many things in my past. That's why I always needed Debbie by my side, to protect me from my own insecurities.

When I finally admitted my problem, Debbie looked surprised, almost skeptical. She didn't know that what she was doing would upset me. You see, I was angry at my wife because I had an unrealistic expectation of her. I thought her job was to stick by my side—always, and literally. Truly, the problem was all mine. I was afraid of people, and because of that problem I had allowed an evil root of bitterness to grow. The bitterness was causing me to snap at Debbie, and if left unchecked it would soon grow wild and cause a host of other problems.

Fortunately, after I admitted my problem to my wife, the healing began—both of my fear of man and the bitterness I felt toward Debbie. Little by little, God began to do a work in me, inviting me to tell Him all my fears, casting them at His feet. As Debbie and I talked through things, I was able to confess before the Lord the bitterness I'd felt toward my wife because of my unmet expectation of her. I was able to allow the Holy Spirit to do the real work in my life, and Debbie and I both were able to forgive each other and reaffirm our love.

Let me ask you a big question—and I encourage you not to answer too quickly. Just think about it for a while.

If something bad or disappointing has happened to you, have you let a root of bitterness grow inside you?

Look at the Root

A root is a cause. In the case of that marital bump, the cause of my anger was my unmet need for security. I was expecting Debbie to fulfill that need, and when she didn't, I let bitterness take root, and I reacted sinfully.

Look at any problem in anyone's life, and the problem is usually exhibited as a symptom that grows from a deeper problem. Say someone is experiencing financial struggles. Usually there is a deeper reason behind those struggles. Or maybe a person goes from one bad relationship to another. There is usually some sort of root or cause why that continues to happen. Perhaps a person can never seem to hold a steady job. Most often there is a cause for that. Some people have issues with fear or anger or addictions. Usually there is a deeper reason behind it.

Bitterness, though, is at the root of all roots. The Bible describes bitterness in Hebrews 12:14–16:

> Pursue peace with all people, and holiness, without which no one will see the Lord: looking carefully lest anyone fall short of the grace of God; lest any root of bitterness springing up cause trouble, and by this many become defiled; lest there be any fornicator or profane person like Esau, who for one morsel of food sold his birthright.

That passage indicates that "many" are able to be defiled by bitterness. It's a serious problem, one that can affect much.

Bitterness—literally—is one of our taste sensations, a sharp, harsh, disagreeable feeling in the mouth. A lemon is bitter. An aspirin tastes bitter before it's swallowed. Bitterness—figuratively—is a disagreeable feeling deep inside us. It's a stinging, piercing sensation inside our souls. Bitterness occurs when we feel life is unfair. We feel offended, pushed aside, annoyed, or provoked. We're resentful, cynical, grieved, jealous, or distressed. We have a chip on our shoulders. We feel we haven't received our fair share. We feel slighted—and it shows.

If we're bitter people, then that bitterness produces other problems. Bitterness comes to a head in a whole host of actions, behaviors, and attitudes of the heart, including addictions, irritability, depression, pornography usage, lust, immorality, anger, a lack of forgiveness, hate, envy, jealousy, and more. Many problems can be traced back to this one root.

I've been there myself. I was saved when I was nineteen, but I was still so close to the world during those first few years of marriage that it was downright hard to live with me. Back then I used to let my frustration turn into anger, and when I got angry, I liked to hit things. By God's grace I never hit Debbie, but I did put a dent in the top of her car once. She joked that I was the Incredible Hulk and needed to watch myself, but I could tell that my actions shook her up.

Another time I became so mad I put a dent in our refrigerator. Debbie put a sunflower magnet over the dent to cover it up, and we went on with our day. But something bigger wasn't right between us—that much was clear.

It wasn't until I dug deeper with the Lord and revealed before Him the source of my anger that things finally began to change. My anger could be traced back to a root of bitterness I had allowed to spring up. One memorable day when I was just a kid, I was bullied by a group of older boys. I was so afraid they were going to hurt me that I started crying—right in the middle of their bullying. They all thought that was a real hoot. They called me names and laughed and mocked me for being a "sissy."

That incident caused a tremendous wound inside me. I felt weak, ashamed, and rejected by others. As a defense, I vowed I would never cry again. From that point on I determined only to act strong and tough—a real Marlboro Man. If something hurt me, I would get angry instead of crying. I turned bitter instead of better, and my bitterness turned into anger. Anger became my default defense mechanism, and unchecked anger has an uncanny way of building to rage. That's why I hit the car and the refrigerator. It took twenty years beyond my childhood for me to be able to cry again. At that point the Lord began to heal me of my childhood wound.

Isaiah 53:5 contains these words of prophecy about Jesus:

He was wounded for our transgressions,
He was bruised for our iniquities;
The chastisement for our peace was upon Him,
And by His stripes we are healed.

Did you catch the sequence? Jesus was wounded and bruised and rejected for us—all so we could be healed—even of this destructive snare. But in order for that to happen, we have to take it seriously.

Bitterness does not have to grow inside our lives. Our wounds and unmet desires can be healed by Christ. We don't have to be bitter people. If bitterness has been allowed to grow, then the bitter root doesn't have to stay. Christ can dig down deeply and remove that root. With the help of the Holy Spirit, we can be truly free.

Bitterness is a spiritual condition that Satan and his bunch can use to trap us in pain and despair. Our job is to prayerfully seek God's face and ask Him to show us this root in our lives. We need to see the truth about this sin, confess it before the Lord, and then ask the Lord in Jesus' name to deliver us from any harmful spiritual oppression that has cropped up around it or because of it. Where there is a void, we should ask God's Holy Spirit to fill our lives anew. Where once was bitterness, pray for healing, forgiveness, cleansing, and restoration.

Let's look at three characteristics of bitter roots—and subsequently at three ways God heals us of bitterness.

#1: Bitter Roots Deceive Us. God Tells Us the Truth.

A root of bitterness can cause great deception in our lives. The demonic spiritual forces that surround bitterness regularly whisper lies into our ears. Because of bitterness we can't see a situation clearly. We aren't able to discern fact from error.

This deception originates from the dawn of time. Paul, in 2 Corinthians 11:3, said, "But I fear, lest somehow, as the serpent deceived Eve by his craftiness, so your minds may be corrupted from the simplicity that is in Christ." Paul reminds us about the original sin committed by Adam and Eve. He warns us that the same thing can happen to us. We, too, can easily be deceived.

Remember the big lie that started it all? Back in Eden, Satan came to Eve and whispered to her, "Go ahead; just eat the fruit." "God knows that in the day you eat of it your eyes will be opened, and you will be like God, knowing good and evil" (Genesis 3:5).

Satan was telling Adam and Eve that if they only would turn away from God, then they would get something they didn't have—if they only would eat the fruit, then their eyes would be opened, and they would be like God. Let me explain that lie.

Adam and Eve already knew *good*. They knew the ultimate embodiment of goodness—in fact, they talked with Him every day. The name of goodness is God. God is the source of all goodness. He is the personification of everything that is right and pure and noble and just and true. God is good. He's always good, all the time.

Satan's lie was that somehow Adam and Eve would be better off if they knew *evil*. Satan was trying to convince them of that: *if only you knew firsthand about evil, then your life would be better.*

How often do we fall into the same trap today?

Satan's demons come to us and whisper that surely God is withholding something from us. Surely God isn't doing something for us that He should be doing. Surely there is something better than what we have. Surely we're missing out on something fun, wild, liberating, satisfying, or exciting.

Satan wants us to believe this lie. He wants us to be bitter toward God.

Mark this carefully. The original sin—not Adam and Eve's but Satan's—was closely associated with bitterness toward God. Isaiah 14 describes how Satan fell: He wanted to be like God because he felt that God was withholding something from him that he deserved. Satan was a splendorous created being who wanted to be as exalted as God.

But God—out of His wisdom, goodness, and justice—said no. That amount of exaltation was to be reserved for God alone. So in his pride and bitterness, Satan rebelled.

There are two ways we believe Satan's lie and fall short of the glory of God—they are two extremes at opposite ends of the spectrum. On one end is lasciviousness, and at the other end is legalism.

Lasciviousness means evil living. It's when people think they can live any way they want and there will be no consequences. For a believer it means trampling underfoot the blood of Christ. As believers we know ultimately that we receive holiness by grace through faith. Yet we are also instructed throughout Scripture to walk in ways that are pleasing to God (2 Corinthians 5:9). If we are not living holy lives, we will not sense the presence of God in our day-to-day activities.

The other way we can fall short is through legalism—we attempt to earn our relationship with God. We work harder and try to shine ourselves up so we look good enough for God. We point to our good works and think that by strictly adhering to a law, principle, or prescription that somehow we will be good enough to be accepted by God. It's *our* works that matter, we insist. Then if we sin or struggle with keeping one of those laws, we judge ourselves unworthy by our unrighteous conduct. Let me tell you: legalists are some of the most miserable people I've ever met. They're always either high on themselves or down on themselves, either proud or crushed.

I met with a couple who told me that for twenty years they had lived close to the poverty level because it was God's will for them to do so. The husband had been fired and had gone from job to job to job. They had gone through bankruptcy, lost a house, drove clunker cars, always depended upon the gifts of others, and were always in need of something.

I asked them why they believed that it was God's will for them to live this way. They told me that God had given them a special word when they were first married. They would always be living hand to mouth because God wanted them to stay dependent on Him.

In my tactful way I said, "That's a lie."

It was a lie because it didn't line up with scripture. Please hear me; there is a *prosperity* gospel that's wrong, but there's a *poverty* gospel that's also wrong. They are two extremes of error and not gospel at all.

The truth is that God *provides* for us. Philippians 4:19 is clear that God supplies all our needs. In Matthew 6:31–32 we're told not to worry about what we eat or wear because our heavenly Father knows that we need these things. James 4:1–2 encourages us to ask God for our necessities. God wants to provide for us so that we can be a blessing to others.

I began to show them in scripture that they had believed a lie. After three or four counseling sessions, they began to admit that they were angry at God. They saw how He was blessing others, but they were bitter that He would not bless them. The problem wasn't God. The problem was that Satan had come in and deceived this couple. They had developed a root of bitterness because of that deception.

Are there any areas of life where we've been deceived? Bitter roots deceive us, whereas God always tells us the truth.

#2: Bitter Roots Defile Many. God Can Cleanse Every Stain.

Look at Hebrews 12:15: "Lest any root of bitterness springing up cause trouble, and by this many become defiled."

This word *defile* is key—in the original language of the text, the word actually means that something is stained or dyed, as with another color.[1] A woman told me recently that every time she looked back on her life, all she could see was a stain. She didn't believe she could ever be happy or at peace because her past was too affected by sin. I told her she was believing a lie, then took her to Isaiah 1:18 and 1 John 1:9, where the blood of Jesus Christ is clearly shown to cleanse us from every sin and stain. Even though our sins are as crimson, they shall be as white as snow.

Note the reference to Esau in Hebrews 12:15–16. We don't want to let any root of bitterness spring up to cause trouble because "by this many become defiled; lest there be any fornicator or profane person like Esau, who for one morsel of food sold his birthright."

Back in Genesis 25:29–34, Esau came in from the fields one day where he'd been hunting, and he was tired and hungry. Esau said to his twin brother Jacob, "Please feed me with that same red stew" (v. 30).

But Jacob wanted to see how much he could get from his brother, so he said, "Sell me your birthright" (v. 31). You see, even though they were twins, Esau was considered the oldest brother because he was the first baby to emerge from the womb. In that culture a birthright gave a son twice what any other sons received for an inheritance. It also meant that the oldest son would become the head of the family after his father died. Blessing and authority were also conveyed upon the holder of the birthright.

Esau squandered his. He said, "Look, I am about to die; so what is this birthright to me?" (v. 32). He was exaggerating. He wasn't about to die. He was just tired and hungry, and he was willing to do anything to have his needs met immediately.

So Jacob traded bread and lentil stew to Esau for the birthright. Esau ate and drank, arose, and went his way as if nothing had happened. Verse 34 says, "Thus Esau despised his birthright." He didn't value it. He traded it all for a meal.

Have you ever wondered what happened next with Esau? It's pretty simple.

He grew bitter.

That bitterness festered and grew. A short time later, as recorded in Genesis 28:6–9,

Esau saw that Isaac had blessed Jacob and sent him away to Padan Aram to take himself a wife from there, and that as he blessed him he gave him a charge, saying, "You shall not take a wife from the daughters of Canaan," and that Jacob had obeyed his father and his mother and had gone to Padan Aram. Also Esau saw that the daughters of Canaan did not please his father Isaac. So Esau went to Ishmael and took Mahalath the daughter of Ishmael, Abraham's son, the sister of Nebajoth, to be his wife in addition to the wives he had.

Esau was trying to hurt his father and mother. If Isaac was displeased with Canaanite wives for his son, then Esau was going to go get one! He was going to do the opposite of whatever made his father happy. Esau allowed a root of bitterness to develop toward his family, and he wanted to hurt his parents any way he could.

Have you ever seen something like this in your own life? Someone has hurt you, so you do something just to spite him? Or maybe it has happened the other way around. You hurt someone, or someone misinterpreted your actions, and your actions offended him, so he did something intentionally to hurt you back.

Please hear me: that sort of action will only destroy people in the end. Usually it will multiply and hurt far more people than ever intended. Bitter roots will also hurt the person who carries them in his heart. Bitterness destroys anyone who holds on to it.

Usually any hurt we feel in our hearts toward a person is ultimately directed at God. That was the pattern that Naomi showed after she lost her husband and two sons in a famine. After she returned home to Bethlehem with her daughter-in-law Ruth, she told the townspeople to call her by a different name. Naomi, her original name, meant "pleasant." But she said, "Call me Mara, for the Almighty has dealt very bitterly with me. I went out full, and the LORD has brought me home again empty. Why do you call me Naomi, since the LORD has testified against me, and the Almighty has afflicted me?" (Ruth 1:20–21). Naomi's new name, Mara, meant "bitter."

That's a root of bitterness directed toward God.

I believe many of us, in our most honest moments, would say something similar to what Naomi said. We look at our lives and there is something for which we blame God. Have you ever said or felt anything like the following?

- God, why is my marriage so difficult? Why don't You do something about it?
- God, why is this person I care so deeply about in such pain? You could heal this person, but You aren't. Why?
- God, why are my children not all I want them to be? You could do something to change their lives, but You aren't. Why?
- God, why is my business suffering? Or, God, why did I lose my job? Or, God, why are we struggling financially?
- God, why isn't my life turning out the way I want it to?

It's certainly okay to ask God difficult questions in prayer, as long as we do so reverently. God is big enough that He can handle anything we ask of Him. But within our questioning we want to make sure that we are not bitter toward God.

The problem of evil and the doctrine of God's sovereignty are both simple and complex at the same time—and they relate directly to any feelings of bitterness we might have toward God. Sovereignty means that God is the supreme ruler of the universe. God has all power over everything. God, in Isaiah 46:9–10 declared, "I am God, and there is no other; I am God, and there is none like Me . . . saying, 'My counsel shall stand, and I will do all My pleasure.'"

Along with the doctrine of sovereignty comes another doctrine: free will. This means that God doesn't want robots, so He allows us to have choices (Romans 6:16). Because of free will, we all—thanks to Adam and Eve—choose to sin. In our world today we have hardship, sickness, struggle, and death. Part of the reason bad things happen is that God has allowed us to make choices. He is still sovereign over everything, yes, but He, in His infinite wisdom, has allowed mankind to live in a fallen world.

Does God's sovereignty mean that God is the author of evil? No. Never. "God is light and in Him is no darkness at all" (1 John 1:5). Yet God still allows evil to exist—and He does so because He is a respecter of mankind's free will. God does not produce evil, yet He permits it. We are asked to have faith that God is still good and that "all things work together for good to those who love God, to those who are the called according to His purpose" (Romans 8:28).

Bitterness turns us away from God. Bitter roots can defile many. The good news is that God can cleanse every stain.

#3: Bitter Roots Depress. God Brings New Life.

Whenever we are bitter, we tend to become downcast or depressed. Bitterness implies that nothing more can be done to remedy a situation, so all that is left is for us to stew in our sorrows. When we carry around bitterness within us, we carry around this sense of discouragement or rejection. This kind of oppression is often something we need to be delivered from in Jesus' name.

This is what happened to Esau. In Hebrews 12:17, Esau later wanted to inherit the blessing, but "he was rejected." He wasn't rejected by God. Rather, Esau carried a sense of rejection within him that allowed him not to receive the blessings of God in his life. Esau continued to carry this sense of rejection, this depression, this discouragement with him, "for he found no place for repentance, though he sought it diligently with tears."

Hebrews 12:16 tells us to watch out for bitterness because it's closely associated with fornication and a profane lifestyle. Fornication is sexual immorality. A profane lifestyle means a person is driven by impure appetites. It could be an appetite for gluttony, lust, violence, greed, or dishonest gain.

A friend of mine, Pastor Olen Griffing, uses an illustration to help us understand this scripture. He says it's like a man who is given an all-expenses-paid trip around the world. The man goes to the airport, eagerly anticipating the trip, and while he waits for the plane, he orders a hamburger. The man is hungry, but the hamburger takes longer to prepare than anticipated. Guess what? The man doesn't let go of the appetite he has for this hamburger. Airline officials give the last call for his flight, but he refuses to get on. Finally he receives and eats his hamburger. But he misses his all-expenses-paid trip. For a moment of pleasure he gives up the opportunity of a lifetime.

Unfortunately we can be just like that man. How many of us have given up our families for a momentary pleasure? How many have given up our businesses for fleeting bits of sin? How many of us have ruined our lives—and the lives of many people we love—all because we believed a lie? Really, any time we sin, we exchange God's pleasure for something far less beneficial to us.

What causes a person to do that? It's a root of bitterness. It's a belief that somehow God is holding out on us. God is not giving us all He has for us.

The Bible is clear about obeying God. Yes, we are given grace when we don't obey Him, but we also are "cursed." Here's the principle in action. Deuteronomy 28 lists out blessings and curses. If we obey God, then blessings generally result. But if we don't obey God, then curses generally result. This principle is repeated in Galatians 6:7: "Whatever a man sows, that he will also reap." Instead of the word *curse*, let me give you a word that's easier for us to grasp—*consequences*. God is not trying to make us feel bad. He's saying that if we obey Him, then good consequences will follow. If we don't obey Him, then bad consequences will follow.

God never haphazardly tells us to obey Him. He always requires obedience for a reason. It's so we will glorify Him, and so our lives will go better. Moses, in Deuteronomy 29:18, told the people to obey God so "that there may not be among you a root bearing bitterness or wormwood."

Ever heard of wormwood?

Literal wormwood is a plant that belongs to the daisy family. It's a strong, bitter herb used for flavoring various dishes, in brewing various alcohols, and as an insect repellent and medicine, particularly as a treatment for malaria. The chemical in wormwood is extremely powerful, and if a person ingests too much wormwood, it causes sickness, convulsions, hallucinations, and various mental problems.

The word *wormwood* is also used figuratively in the Bible. Solomon says in Proverbs that if someone goes after an immoral woman, it's like wormwood, producing a poison that will kill (5:3–4).

C. S. Lewis's *The Screwtape Letters* is a satirical apologetic written in story form to help unbelievers understand the Bible. In the book, Screwtape was the name given to a demon who wrote letters to his nephew, a young demon named Wormwood, telling him how to corrupt people and tempt them away from God. Lewis got the name Wormwood from a biblical reference—Revelation 8:10–11:

> Then the third angel sounded: And a great star fell from heaven, burning like a torch, and it fell on a third of the rivers and on the springs of water. The name of the star is Wormwood. A third of the waters became wormwood, and many men died from the water, because it was made bitter.

What's the point?

Bitterness sickens people, even kills them. Bitterness is a poison in our systems that must be removed by deliverance, confession, forgiveness, and prayer.

Finally Free from Bitterness

I've had my own experiences with bitterness—both with bitterness I've felt personally and with bitterness in my family.

When Gateway began to grow so rapidly, it felt as if everything exploded. As the church began to become known both nationally and internationally, we became a lead church in the body of Christ. Simultaneously, I wrote books and spoke at other churches. With this type of quick success came a busyness that soon proved overwhelming.

One of the causalities of that busyness was my daughter. When I began to get so incredibly busy, she was in her key mid-teen years— thirteen to fifteen, an impressionable age of life—and I really failed her during that time by not being around as much as I needed to be.

This caused a root of bitterness to grow in her. She became angry at me, God, and the church because, in her own words, "the church stole my dad." She began to live in sin. For several years we all struggled because of this.

When she was about eighteen years old, I began to realize as I was praying for her that my actions had harmed my daughter. I knew I needed to repent. One day I had a long conversation with her and told her how sorry I was. We both cried. I said, "Sugar, the resentment that you feel toward me is valid. I'm so sorry for neglecting you. I'm the one who was wrong. But you have a responsibility here too. Please choose to forgive me. If you don't, then the bitterness that you feel will destroy your life."

She forgave me, and I watched God pull a root of bitterness out of her. Within a few weeks of that, she repented. Today she is in her mid-twenties and a conference speaker who helps many others get rid of this root of bitterness.

There's one important question left in this study. One of the main difficulties with overcoming bitterness is that if a person has hurt us, and that person never asks for forgiveness, then we feel we can't forgive that person. What do we do then?

The answer is that we do what Jesus did. We forgive anyway.

When Jesus was on the cross, one of His final statements was that He was thirsty, and people gave Him vinegar to drink. Have you ever wondered why they gave Him a bitter drink and not regular wine? It's because they wanted everything to be as harsh for Him as possible. A drink of vinegar might slake His thirst and keep Him alive for a while longer so He would suffer more. The people who crucified Jesus were never going to ask for forgiveness from Him. The last drink He received was very possibly an indication of Christ's last temptation—to be bitter at them. To hold a grudge.

Not only did Jesus not drink the bitter drink, but He said, "Father, forgive them." Jesus made a choice to forgive and not to be bitter.

The same choice is ours.

Is there resentment in your life? Is there unchecked anger, hurt, disappointment, or disillusionment? This bitterness will eat away at your life. You need to forgive. Perhaps there is a person, group of people, or institution you need to forgive. Perhaps you need to forgive yourself. After I was involved with immorality, it took years of God's mercy before I was able to forgive myself for the pain I inflicted on my family and others. Perhaps you need to forgive God. That might sound strange because God cannot sin. Yet the word *forgive* simply means "release." You release God. You say, "God, I know that this happened to me, and I'm not going to hold You responsible for this anymore. I know it wasn't You who did it to me. By faith I believe that You always love me and always have my best interest in mind."

Let me pray for us here as we close this chapter.

Holy Spirit of God, please pull any root of bitterness out of our hearts. We say before You that life hasn't always worked out the way we hoped it would, and because of that we have allowed bitterness to form. Right now, in prayer, we want to release anybody or anything that we have been holding a grudge against. We release that person or thing. By Your power and might, we choose to forgive. Deliver us now, in Jesus' name, from any demonic strongholds that may have been caused by this bitterness. We agree in prayer that our lives belong to You, Jesus Christ, and that we will follow You wholeheartedly. Fill us now with all the fullness, goodness, and power of God's Holy Spirit. We ask these things in the strong name of Jesus Christ, amen.

Questions for Contemplation or Group Discussion

1. When a person speaks with resentment, does he or she seem like a resentful person overall? Do you think it's possible to be resentful in just one area of life?

2. Esau was driven by appetite, and we live in a world that thrives on instant gratification. What ways do you tend to give in easily to the satisfaction in front of you instead of relying on the Lord?

3. Naomi said, "Call me Mara, for the Almighty has dealt very bitterly with me" (Ruth 1:20). What would you have said to Naomi? How would you respond to a person who says, "God did this to me"?

4. How does it make you feel when someone who has hurt you is blessed by the Lord? What is God's perception of that person? What does God think about the situation you experienced?

5. Think of a person who grew up experiencing a lot of relationships with resentment. Describe what that person's life would be like if the root of bitterness was removed. How might this person's life change? How might this person's perception of God change?

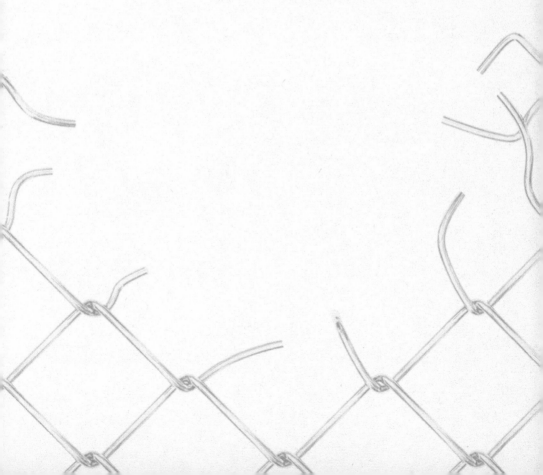

Chapter Six

BREAKING THE
SNARE OF GREED

Give, and it will be given to you: good measure,
pressed down, shaken together,
and running over will be put into your bosom.
For with the same measure that you use,
it will be measured back to you.

—LUKE 6:38

I was speaking at a conference, and before I went onstage to speak, the leader in charge of the event asked me—his wording was quite specific—if I would *receive* the offering.

Inwardly I chuckled, and not unkindly. He was a younger leader and well-intentioned. Besides, this is the type of wording that's often used in Christian churches immediately before passing a plate. He had undoubtedly picked it up from someone else and was just repeating what he'd learned. But for the sake of raising a quick conversation about the nature of giving, I decided I'd have just a bit of fun with him.

"Well, sure," I said. "I'd love to receive the offering from a crowd this large."

He looked puzzled, shook his head, and said, "Oh no, I didn't mean that you would receive it personally. I meant"—and here his wording was again specific—"will you *take* the offering?"

"Absolutely I'll take the offering," I said. "Where would you like me to take it?"

He opened his mouth, but no words came out. Then he squinted as if I belonged in an insane asylum.

Finally I let him off the hook. "You're asking me to lead the people in giving tonight, right?"

"Yeah." He smiled in relief. "Would you?"

My point was a simple one, yet it has large implications for every believer. That discussion about wording highlighted one of the most misunderstood principles in Christianity. Church leaders don't *receive* offerings, and we don't *take* offerings.

Instead, we *give* offerings, and we *bring* them to God.

Let me expand upon this principle and state it again more strongly, this time with a warning behind it. Christians *must* bring offerings to God. If we don't, then our reasons for not doing so can be problematic in big ways.

Throughout my years in pastoral ministry, I've seen this play out again and again. If we close every door to the enemy in our lives yet we don't give to God, then we've left open one large door for the enemy to attack us.

A Tough—Yet Necessary—Subject

In spite of that warning, I suspect you might want to skip this chapter and jump to the next. I can almost hear the audible groan. "There goes another preacher asking for money. And this time he's backing it up with a warning of spiritual oppression." You might even suspect I'm only including this chapter so I can get more money for my church.

I assure you, that is the farthest thing from the truth.

I teach about the necessity of giving to God because it's a principle found throughout the Bible. I lay the subject out before you with great reverence for God and, I hope, with great sensitivity to you. In fact, if you're still groaning audibly about this subject, here are three things I'd like you to know.

First, for most of my ministry I've hesitated to approach the topic of money. In fact, I had been a preacher for several years before I ever preached a sermon about giving. By then I had preached on just about every other biblical topic—marriage, prayer, forgiveness, grace, you name it. But I never wanted to be seen as self-serving. Then after ten years I finally realized I was doing people a disservice by neglecting this important topic. I needed to preach on everything that Scripture addresses, and Scripture actually talks a lot about money. That's why I'm bringing up the subject here.

Second, some pastors preach about giving every time they stand in front of a microphone. But at Gateway Church I address the subject only every two to three years because I know how sensitive people can be about money. While I've come to believe that giving is important, it's not as important as the main thing we focus on at our church—the glory of God in the gospel. I always want the reconciliatory ministry of Jesus Christ to have preeminence.

Third, at Gateway I'm so careful about broaching this subject that we don't even pass an offering plate during our services. Instead, we have drop boxes near the entrance doors, where people can leave the offerings they've brought. Now, church-growth statisticians will tell you that if you're trying to generate the maximum offering you can from your congregation, drop boxes are not the way to go. They're too easy to overlook or pass by. But I deliberately use the drop boxes because I want all giving at Gateway to be motivated by love for God and given freely from the heart, not prompted by passing a plate or under compulsion (2 Corinthians 9:7 NIV).[1]

And do you know what? By God's grace we have never suffered from a financial lack at Gateway. Last year alone the people in our church gave to the Lord so abundantly that we gave away more than a million dollars each month to missions.

God, Love, and Money

Let's look again at the distinctions I mentioned at the beginning of the chapter. We must make a fundamental shift in our minds if we are to understand this issue correctly.

Again, churches don't *receive* offerings. Rather, Christians freely *give* them and *bring* them to God.

All this may sound like mere semantics, but it's not. Our money is already God's (1 Corinthians 10:26). When we bring our money to Him, "he is not served by human hands, as if he needed anything. Rather, he himself gives everyone life and breath and everything else" (Acts 17:25 NIV). So since God already owns everything, there are only two things we can do with our money, according to the Bible—we can either bring our tithes and offerings to God's house, or we can rob God of what is His.

Think of it this way. Imagine you're going out of town next week. You inform your next-door neighbor about your trip and he says, "Hey, this is great timing. I need to get my car fixed, and they don't give out loaner cars at the mechanic's shop I like. Would you mind if I borrowed your truck while you're away? I'll even drop you off at the airport."

It's a reasonable request. Your neighbor is a good guy. You drive a Toyota truck, and it's sturdy and reliable. So you say, "Well, of course you can borrow my truck."

The day of your trip arrives. Your neighbor drops you off at the airport in your Toyota and wishes you well. At the end of the week, he returns to the airport in your Toyota truck, picks you up, hands back your keys, and says, "Hey, I've done some thinking while you were away, and because I'm so generous, I've decided I'm not going to keep this truck for myself. I'd like you to receive this Toyota truck from me. Take it. The truck is yours to keep."

What would you do? You'd probably think your neighbor was just joking, or perhaps you'd wonder if he was a little touched in the head. You'd definitely want to clarify that he's only *returning* your truck. He's not doing you any favors. The truck was yours in the first place.

Yet this very same dynamic occurs all too often between us and God. We may not actually say it, but our basic attitude is "God, because I'm so generous, I'd like to drop this cash in the offering plate this week. Here You go. Enjoy."

Sorry. It doesn't work that way.

We can't give away what doesn't belong to us. It was already God's money to begin with—He loaned it to us. When we bring our offerings, all we're doing is returning back to God what He has graciously let us use.

It's imperative we grasp this core principle—that everything in our hands already belongs to God. Once we do so, we are able to ask the next important question: If God already owns everything, then why does He tell people in Scripture to bring Him offerings?

The wonder here is that when we let Scripture answer this question for us, we can see anew how much God loves us. Even the money we bring to Him is tied into His great love for us.

Why Give?

The simplest, most basic answer is that God said so. From the early days of His covenant with Israel, God's children have been instructed to set aside a portion of their blessings—called a tithe—to do God's work.

I mention this point right up front because I know some Bible teachers disagree with me about what Scripture says about giving. They accuse me of misapplying Old Testament verses to New Testament situations, and they insist that the word *tithe* isn't even mentioned in the New Testament.

That's okay. The criticism doesn't bother me personally, and I know I'll meet these brothers in heaven one day, and we'll all shake hands about the subject then.

The word *tithe*, if you're new to church, simply means a tenth. In the Old Testament, God's people were repeatedly instructed to return one-tenth of their income to the Lord. Leviticus 27:30 states, "And all the tithe of the land, whether of the seed of the land or of the fruit of the tree, is the LORD's."

In the *New* Testament the word *tithe* appears *eight times*. (I don't know how scholars can miss that, but apparently they do!) And the New Testament is full of other references to the importance of giving. Here are just a few.

- Throughout the Gospels, Jesus repeatedly shows people that God is their provider and that they don't need to worry about material possessions. (For instance, see Matthew 6:24–34 and Luke 21:1–4.)
- In 1 Corinthians 16:1–2, the early church is seen regularly collecting funds at its worship services. Paul treated this giving as if it were normative, as it should be.
- In 2 Corinthians 9:7, every believer is instructed to give cheerfully.
- In Galatians 6:6, those who are taught the Word are instructed to share "in all good things" with those who teach.
- In Ephesians 4:28, believers are taught to give to those who are in need.
- In 1 Timothy 5:17–18, the church is instructed to financially support its ministers.

The Right Motives

There are other reasons to give, of course, but we need to be careful in considering them. If we say, "Give because we're bound to receive an even bigger reward in return," then we're misguided. Too many Bible teachers lead with this teaching. They insist that if we give to God, then we will *get* from God—and in a big way. "You can't outgive God," they say, and that's true in a sense, but it can also be distorted to make tithing sound like a get-rich-quick scheme.

The problem is that if we give only to get, our motivation for giving becomes skewed. We give to God only in hopes that God will increase our bank accounts. That's nothing more than greed, and it can lead to disappointment and disillusionment.

James 4:3 hones in on this issue from another angle: "When you ask, you do not receive, *because you ask with wrong motives*, that you may spend what you get on your pleasures" (NIV). In other words, we must always interact with God with right motives if we want to please Him.

Motives matter because giving is really an issue of the heart. The heart is always what matters to God. If we want to please Him and operate in line with His kingdom principles, we must offer our tithes with right motives.

But what are the right motives for giving? We give because we want to honor God. We're invited to bring a portion of what He's given us back to Him so we can be part of His awesome kingdom plans.

Our reward for giving only comes because we have allowed God to do a work in our hearts in the area of giving—not in the area of getting. In God's economy it's always the giving that matters—the giving, the giving, the giving. Not the getting. God invites us to give because giving is good for us. Any increase we receive is only a by-product of the giving.

Think of it from a parental standpoint. Have you ever seen young children at Christmastime? Sure, it's a season of splendor and delight, of fun and wonder. Yet there is almost always a display of their greed as well. Children are eager to create massive wish lists, to closely scrutinize the presents under the tree, and to rip open presents on Christmas morning.

We expect this of children because they are immature. But if our children are adults in their twenties, thirties, or forties and still behave this way, then we have a problem. We hope they have grown up by then and learned to be less selfish. We are elated when they enjoy blessing others. And we delight in seeing that they have grown to become cheerful, willing givers.

This maturity is what God calls us to as well. He forms and shapes us to become cheerful, abundant, unselfish, faithful givers. The apostle Paul spelled out what maturity looks like in the area of giving in 2 Corinthians 9:6–8:

He who sows sparingly will also reap sparingly, and he who sows bountifully will also reap bountifully. So let each one give as he purposes in his heart, not grudgingly or of necessity; for God loves a cheerful giver. And God is able to make all grace abound toward you, that you, always having all sufficiency in all things, may have an abundance for every good work.

It's a beautiful picture, isn't it? But for most of us, the issue of money and material possessions is closely intertwined with issues of trust, self-worth, priorities, and sin, which is why we sometimes get tripped up in this important area of Christian maturity. As I mentioned at the start of this chapter, confusion or disobedience in returning to God what's already His can open the door to spiritual oppression.

Let's look at a couple of ways this can happen and what can be done if it does.

Tripping Point #1: Unbelief

In the third chapter of Malachi, in the midst of a passage that discusses giving, God speaks:

> *Yet from the days of your fathers*
> *You have gone away from My ordinances,*
> *And have not kept them.* (v. 7)

The word *ordinance* means a law or rule that governs everyday living. (The word *ordinary* comes from the same root.) A city today, for instance, might have an ordinance against littering. Tithing was one of God's ordinances—an expected part of everyday Israelite living. It was normal for God's people to learn to return what belongs to God.

Repeat: the tithe belongs to God. That's normal. Period. In the particular case of Malachi 3, the Israelites had fallen off from this practice, and God was rebuking them for it.

God went on to explain how they had actually robbed Him by

not bringing the whole tithe to Him (v. 8). For this reason, they were "cursed" (v. 9). This spiritual curse was fleshed out physically for them as well. God's people lacked food (v. 10), and their crops were being destroyed (v. 11).

That's the bad news, but here's the good news as well. God also offered a solution for their unbelieving hearts. He challenged them to "try" Him in the area of giving. If they would bring in the whole tithe, then He would

> *open for you the windows of heaven*
> *And pour out for you such blessing*
> *That there will not be room enough to receive it.* (v. 10)

It's amazing to me how many people today try to overlook this scripture or explain it away by insisting the passage has no relevance anymore. Yes, God was specifically addressing the people of Israel in this passage. Yet in the very same chapter of Malachi, God said, "For I am the LORD, I do not change" (v. 6). The principle of honoring God with our money is timeless.

The big question the Israelites were wrestling with in this passage was unbelief. Did they believe that God would bless them if they gave? Did they believe they would still have enough for themselves?

How like us today. Have you ever found yourself struggling with questions like that? They're important to work through because they have powerful spiritual implications.

In the next verse God made a promise:

> *And I will rebuke the devourer for your sakes,*
> *So that he will not destroy the fruit of your ground.* (v. 11)

Awhile back I read a footnote in a certain Bible translation that speculated the "devourer" was probably some sort of natural blight that had come on the land. Wrong. (By the way, footnoted commentary in Bibles is not inspired by the Lord; footnotes are only the opinions of scholars.)

In this passage "the devourer" is actually a reference to spiritual oppression. God was saying, "If you believe in Me and honor Me by giving as I have ordained, I will close the door to Satan's attack on your life so you can flourish and be fruitful."

The principle of honoring God with our finances is an eternal principle that runs throughout the Word of God, from Genesis to Revelation. God wants us to learn to give and give cheerfully—not under compulsion and not under law (Romans 6:14), but as a matter of faith—honoring God with the money He has entrusted to us because we believe in Him and want to be part of what He is doing.

If we choose not to do that—if we close every door in our lives but don't honor God's giving principles, then we've left a door open to the enemy. We are not trusting in God as our Provider. Our stingy attitudes are symptoms of unbelief, and this in turn makes us vulnerable to attack.

Tripping Point #2: Fear

Time and time again I meet two groups of people. The first group tithes. The second group does not. Every tither I have ever spoken with has given me a similar testimony. Every nontither has also given me a similar testimony—one that is very different from those who tithe. Interestingly both groups are composed of people from every socioeconomic background. It's not the upper-income bracket that tithes and the lower-income bracket that doesn't. There are always folks from across the economic spectrum in each group.

Without exception the tithers say, "I'm blessed, or "God has blessed me."

Without exception the nontithers say, "I can't afford to tithe," or "I don't have enough money to tithe."

What's happening here?

It's the principle of firstfruits in action—the principle that whatever comes to us, we must give the first portion of it back to God.

Proverbs 3:9–10 says,

> Honor the LORD with your possessions,
> And with the firstfruits of all your increase;
> So your barns will be filled with plenty,
> And your vats will overflow with new wine.[2]

The word *honor* is key in that verse. We're instructed to honor the Lord with our possessions. Elsewhere in the Bible the word *honor* is expounded. God, in 1 Samuel 2:30 said, "For those who honor Me I will honor." Jesus repeated this principle in John 12:26: "If anyone serves Me, him My Father will honor."

If we don't hold to this biblical principle, then we're living in fear. We are basically saying to God, "I'm afraid that if I give to You, I won't have enough left over for myself. Sorry, but I can't honor You with my possessions."

Consider this. In the Bible there are more than five hundred verses that deal with prayer and roughly the same amount that deal with faith. That sounds like a lot—but did you know that there are more than *two thousand* verses on the subject of money and possessions? Jesus talked about money in sixteen of His thirty-eight parables.

Clearly, we need to understand what money is all about and how to handle it, because the way we use our money reveals the condition of our heart. We put money toward what we value most. Money is actually a test from God.

A test? Absolutely.

Remember that *tithe* means a tenth, or 10 percent of our income. Now, some may find this coincidental, but I don't: the number ten is used throughout Scripture to indicate testing. Ask yourself these questions.

How many times did God test Pharaoh's heart with plagues (Exodus 7:14–12:30)?

Ten.

How many main commandments did God give the people of Israel through Moses (Exodus 20:1–17)?

Ten.

How many times did the Israelites test God when they wandered in the wilderness (Numbers 14:20–25)?

Ten.

How many times were Jacob's wages changed (Genesis 31:7)?

Ten.

How many days were Daniel and his three friends tested (Daniel 1:12–14)?

Ten.

How many virgins were tested in Matthew 25:1–13?

Ten.

How many days of testing are mentioned in Revelation 2:10?

Ten.

How many disciples did Jesus call?

Twelve. (I was just testing to see if you were still with me.)

Whenever we get paid or receive money, God is testing us. The test is to see whom we will honor. Whom will we thank? Whom will we point to and worship as the Giver of all good gifts?

Will we believe that 90 percent with God's financial blessing will actually go farther than 100 percent of it without His blessing? That's part of the test. God wants to remind us that we can live either by faith or by fear. Which would you rather choose?

The sequence is important. We are called to give away our firstfruits before we know if we have enough to live on. We are called to give to God first because we are called to live by faith. And, as my faithful group of tithers will testify, God always comes through. When we give this way, we always see the blessings of God.

Adventures in Fearless Finances

I receive my salary from the church on the fifteenth and the last day of the month—either the thirtieth or the thirty-first. My paycheck is deposited automatically in my account. So here's what I do. On that morning, while I'm having my quiet time, I go online, and I send my tithe to the church. My tithe is the first portion of money that leaves my account after the paycheck arrives. Debbie and I have chosen to give 20 percent. I don't mention this to brag; it's just something God has called us to do since 1984. We give over and above that to various ministries, but the first 20 percent always goes directly to the local church as a way to honor God with our finances.

Some will frown at this point and say, "Yeah, Pastor Robert, but you have no financial worries. You have a steady job. What about those who don't?"

It doesn't matter if you're on minimum wage or a billionaire. God always calls us to trust Him to provide. I haven't always had a steady job. I mentioned that 1984 was a significant year for Debbie and me, the year we began trusting God at another level. In those days I was working as a traveling evangelist, and money was extremely tight for us. We didn't draw a consistent paycheck back then. We'd drive to any place that called me to preach, and the people there would give us an offering. We might receive eight hundred dollars one month and two hundred dollars the next. We never knew for sure how much it would be.

Fortunately we were already tithers. We'd been tithing for several years in our marriage, and God had impressed upon us that we were never to worry about money, even without a consistent paycheck— money would always be there.

One day we pulled up to a gas station in our rickety old station wagon. We were in the middle of Oklahoma—I don't even remember the town. But I remember very clearly what happened at that gas station. I filled our car and walked inside to pay. The woman behind the counter said, "No charge. It's taken care of."

"Excuse me?" I asked. I didn't quite catch what she was saying.

"Your gasoline has been paid for," she said. "When you pulled up, God told me that you were an evangelist and that I was to pay for your gas. I obeyed God. There's no charge for you."

Another time during that same year I preached at a church and they gave me a particularly large sum of money as a thank-you gift. This one check would cover all our expenses for the month. But as I stood there holding the check, I felt a distinct impression I was to sign over this entire check to a missionary who'd spoken at the same church earlier in the evening. I wrestled in prayer for a few moments, then decided to obey God. I didn't tell anybody about my decision. In fact, I endorsed the check secretly and handed it to the missionary with a specific instruction for him not to tell anybody. I wasn't sure how Debbie and I were going to pay our bills that month, but I wasn't worried. God would provide.

Later that same evening, a group of church members took us out to eat at a nearby pizza parlor. One of the members took me aside and asked me to tell him the exact amount of money I'd received that night as a gift. The question shook me up a little, and I stalled at first, but eventually I told him. I remember his words exactly: "God is about to teach you about giving so you can teach the body of Christ." He handed me a folded check. It was already made out, and it was ten times the amount—to the penny—of the check I'd just given away.

A few weeks after that, I spoke at an in-home Bible study where one of the couples was about to go overseas as missionaries. As we were praying for them, I received the distinct impression that they still needed eight hundred dollars. They'd never revealed this amount to me or to anyone in the group that I knew of, but the figure of eight hundred dollars was clear in my mind. Because of the large sum I'd just received from the man at the pizza parlor, I wrote a check for the full eight hundred and handed it over to the missionaries. Big grins came over their faces. It was the precise amount they still needed.

Not long after that I went out to lunch with a man who'd just purchased a brand-new van. It was worth more than twenty-five thousand dollars, and when lunch was over, he handed me the keys, saying it was a gift for Debbie and me.

I couldn't believe it. We had two cars now, and while we could certainly use a second car, something didn't feel quite right about keeping both vehicles. Our station wagon had high miles, yet it was reliable, and there was a lot of life still left in it. Debbie and I prayed about it and believed the Lord was instructing us to give away our second car. So we gave away our station wagon to a family that needed a vehicle.

Right after that, someone gave us a different second car. We were happy. We had a second car again. Then we prayed about it and felt that God was calling us to give that one away too. So we did.

Not long afterward, someone gave us yet another second car.

We gave that one away too.

We received yet another car in return.

We gave that one away—and received another one.

Over the course of eighteen months, this happened nine times!

Finally, with one of the vehicles we felt a distinct impression that God was telling us not to give this one away. He wanted us to sell this vehicle. In fact, in prayer, we believed we were supposed to sell it for a specific price—twelve thousand dollars.

We didn't tell anybody about the decision to sell the vehicle or how much we were asking for the car. But the next weekend at church, a man walked up to us and, out of the blue, asked us if we wanted to sell the vehicle. We said yes, and right away he offered us twelve thousand dollars.

We accepted and put the money in the bank, not sure what to do with it. Soon after that, Debbie and I went on a short-term mission trip to Costa Rica. A missionary picked us up and drove us around in an old van. At one point I asked him if he was in the market for a new vehicle.

"Last week I was driving by a car lot," he said, "and the Lord told me to stop. The Lord pointed out a van to me and said, *This van will be yours. Pray over it.* So I did, but nothing has happened so far. I don't have the money for it. I'm trusting the Lord to provide. Why do you ask?"

"How much do they want for the van?" I asked.

"It's used," he said. "They want twelve thousand for it."

I wrote him a check.

Debbie and I have story after story like that of times when we've believed the Lord has called us to give something away—sometimes cash, sometimes a specific material possession. Once we learned not to fear, it became fun. And God has always provided for us, always abundantly more than we've ever given away.

Hope When We're Tempted to Doubt God

Giving is good for us. Giving honors God, and God promises to honor us when we honor Him.

By contrast, not giving is problematic for us. If we don't believe that God will provide for us or if we're afraid to test Him in this, then that fear or lack of trust can open doors to the enemy's influence.

That's the way Satan operates. Right from the dawn of time, he has tried to convince men and women to doubt God's Word. God gave Adam and Eve permission to eat the fruit of every tree in the garden of Eden except one. This one tree was called "the tree of the knowledge of good and evil." God told Adam and Eve, "the day that you eat of it you shall surely die" (Genesis 2:17).

Did God say that because the fruit of that tree was poisonous?

No. Everything God had created was good (Genesis 1:31). Rather, God gave Adam and Eve that command as a test. He had reserved one tree out of all the others in the garden for Himself alone. Only that one tree was not intended for Adam and Eve. But could He trust them to obey His word? And could they trust Him to bless them and care for them?

Satan directly contradicted God's word, however, and Adam and Eve failed the test. The pattern for mistrusting God was established.

That's what Satan wants to happen to us today. He wants us to doubt God.

When the serpent approached Eve in the garden of Eden, he said, in essence, "Did God really say what you think He said? You must have heard Him wrong. Surely you can eat the fruit from *all* the trees. After all, everything God has given you is yours."

Let me ask you this: Why did Eve desire the fruit from the one tree from which she couldn't eat? There were many other beautiful trees in the garden of Eden. Surely she wasn't hungry. The garden was a perfect environment for humankind. God had fully provided for her.

Genesis 2:9 gives us the clue as to why: "Out of the ground the LORD God made every tree grow that is *pleasant* to the sight and good for food. The tree of life was also in the midst of the garden, and the tree of the knowledge of good and evil."

All the trees in the garden were pleasant looking. All of them, even the one that was forbidden. Eve had everything she needed. She simply wanted more. Her sin was greed.

God's holding out on me, she thought. *He told us we can't have it all. But I want it all.* Eve wanted more and more nice things, and it's okay for people to want nice things. But nice should come from God's blessing, not from robbing God. God blesses us when we believe His Word. God blesses us when we live by faith. When He tells us to do something and we do it, then we're blessed. But Adam and Eve took what belonged to God.

Do you see the connection between Adam and Eve and our lives today? God gives us a similar test. He invites us to trust Him in the area of giving. If we do so, He is honored, and the blessing is ours. It's that simple.

Let's pray together.

Lord God, we want to believe what You say in Your Word. You invite us to trust You, to give generously and bless others through giving. All we have is Yours anyway. Forgive us our unbelief, our fear, and our greed. In the name of Jesus Christ, remove any spiritual oppression we may be experiencing due to these sins. We don't want to give the devourer any open doors in our lives. From this day forward we choose to be wholehearted and cheerful givers. We give because we honor You. You are Lord over our lives. You care for us deeply. From this moment on, please give us Your peace in the area of giving. We ask this in the strong name of Jesus Christ, God almighty, amen.

I had an older man tell me once that he'd never been a tither but he wanted to start. He asked if he should calculate his debt over the years and try to pay back the Lord. I think a lot of people wonder about the same thing. I'll tell you what I told him that day: I said no. Jesus has paid it all for you—that's the wonder of God's grace in our lives. Jesus wiped the slate clean. Just respond to His grace. Repent and start fresh today by closing this door and doing what's right.

We've been making some strong progress in this study so far. I hope we've been able to reveal—and then close—some open doors to spiritual oppression. But we're not finished yet. The next chapter covers one of the major doors through which Satan can enter our lives. In fact, this problem is so prevalent today that I considered placing this next chapter at the start of the book. I refrained because I was concerned it would overshadow the rest of the book. But we do need to address the issue because leaving this door open can cause us big trouble.

In the meantime, be encouraged. A big problem lies ahead. But so does big hope!

Questions for Contemplation or Group Discussion

1. How did you first learn about tithing? Over the past few years, have you had a positive or negative perspective on it?

2. Read Genesis 3:1–6. Eve thought that something besides what God had given her would make her happy. How is this similar to our own thinking? What are some ways we want "more," even as we are abundantly blessed?

3. How does tithing close the door to greed, unbelief, and fear?

4. Read Malachi 3:6–12. This passage contains a confrontation and a promise. What does it tell us about God's character and His heart for us?

5. Do you have a story about how tithing changed your life or the life of someone else? Share it with the group or write it down in a journal.

Chapter Seven

BREAKING THE
SNARE OF LUST

Put on the Lord Jesus Christ, and make no provision for the flesh, to fulfill its lusts.

—ROMANS 13:14

The temptation to lust is huge today.

As I mentioned earlier in this book, I've struggled with it, and a time came early in my ministry when I realized I was in bondage in this area. Yes, I was a Christian when this happened, even in ministry. I preached sermons, prayed for people, and counseled people in God's Word. I led people regularly to salvation in Jesus Christ. But I still had this problem, and I wasn't telling anybody about it because of fear and shame.

My problem came to a head when I was thirty. I had struggled off and on with the lure of pornography and sexual immorality since I was twelve. Mostly I'd tried to resist this problem with my willpower, but that never seemed to do much good, and my good intentions rarely lasted. When I became a believer at age nineteen, I hoped my problems with lust would go away. They didn't. More than a decade later, I was still battling this same difficulty, still trying to fight that sin with my willpower alone. And I was losing big-time.

One weekend, three of us pastors were scheduled to speak at a conference. On Friday night I preached my session, then went back to my hotel room. More sessions were scheduled for Saturday morning, Saturday night, and Sunday morning. I was tired and yet I couldn't sleep, so I flipped on the TV and started channel surfing. One small glance at a snippet of salacious material led to a second, longer glance, and soon I was reveling in something I had no business watching. I returned to my sin as a dog returns to his vomit (Proverbs 26:11).

The next morning I phoned my wife and confessed to her the previous night's carnality. I wanted to be open with Debbie and open to the people around me who could help hold me accountable. Now, accountability is a really good thing in general, and I invite anyone struggling with this same problem to be accountable to other trusted believers. But as good as accountability is as a general principle, it didn't set me free in this case. I continued with the conference, and all the while I had a sick feeling in my stomach. I was still in bondage. I needed to be set free.

On Sunday morning I sat in the main auditorium and wondered what to do. One of the other pastors preached, and it was as if a bright light had switched on. He preached about the reality of believers being held in bondage, and his message seemed tailor-made for me. As the message progressed, I kept thinking, *This is me! This is me! This is me!*

At the end he gave an invitation, saying, "God wants to set you free today, but you need to humble yourself." He invited people to come forward for prayer and deliverance. I was seated right on the front row, and at first I felt a momentary twinge of pride. What would it look like to other people if a pastor went forward? But the Holy Spirit was speaking directly to my heart, saying, *This is it, Robert. This is for you.* That was all the nudge I needed. I was the very first one standing at the front of the room, praying for deliverance. So I want you to know I'm writing this chapter from the place of a person who understands what it is like to be in bondage to this.

Here's the good news. Jesus set me free, and He can set you free too. The spirit of lust has undoubtedly destroyed more people's lives than any other spirit, but that does not have to happen.

This is such a big subject I want to take two chapters to cover it. In this chapter I'll give more of a general overview. Then, in the chapter to come, I'll talk about one of the specific struggles that goes hand in hand with lust—the battle for our thought lives.

Stay with me here. There are good things ahead.

A Primer for Wise Living

About three thousand years ago, King Solomon witnessed a disturbing incident in his city. Through the inspiration of the Holy Spirit, he wrote it down as a warning to others to avoid similar situations. The seventh chapter of Proverbs offers a powerful glimpse into how the spirit of lust operates, and Solomon's warning can be highly useful for our benefit and instruction today. Let's walk through the chapter in depth.

Solomon began by exhorting his listeners to live wise and prudent lives. This needs to be our goal as believers today too. Wise living is seldom touted in popular culture, yet the Bible has not changed its exhortation over time. "Treasure my commands within you," Solomon wrote:

> *Keep my commands and live . . .*
> *That they may keep you from the immoral woman,*
> *From the seductress who flatters with her words.* (vv. 1–2, 5)

As you can see, Solomon wrote specifically to a male audience, namely, his son. Yet imprudent and immoral living is not reserved for men alone, and these biblical commands apply to women as well. Although Solomon spoke about the danger posed by a "seductress," the problem he surfaced was actually the spirit of lust, which can influence both genders.

Beginning in Proverbs 7:6, Solomon described looking out a window and spotting "a young man devoid of understanding" (v. 7). He was not slighting young people here, just describing a particular young person who failed to live a wise and prudent life. Already the young man was in the wrong place at the wrong time—and he'd placed himself there by choice.

Why would anyone intentionally put himself in harm's way? It's because the spirit of lust robs people of wisdom and understanding. When under the influence of this spirit, people act in illogical ways. I see this all the time in people bound to lust. When people actually think through their actions, they know what they're doing is wrong, yet they continue to do it. The apostle Paul described this logical disconnect in Romans 7:15: "For I do not understand my own actions. For I do not do what I want, but I do the very thing I hate" (ESV).

How does this illogical behavior pan out? In Proverbs 7:8–9, we see the dangerous choice the young man made:

> *Passing along the street near her corner . . .*
> *He took the path to her house*
> *In the twilight, in the evening,*
> *In the black and dark night.*

The young man knew exactly what he was doing, foolish though his actions were. He was walking toward the house of a harlot, and he was doing so under the cover of night.

Walking toward evil at night makes for a deadly combination, yet how often does something similar happen today? A man will drive his car into the red-light district of town, all the while telling himself that he just wants to "take a new route home." Or he'll "check his e-mail" on his computer late in the evening when he's tired and feeling lonely, knowing full well he's only one click away from immorality. Or a woman will spend too much time mulling the pictures on an old boyfriend's Facebook page, fantasizing about what had transpired between them or what could be if only they connected again. They're all treading into areas of extreme danger!

We cannot give the enemy a foothold into our lives like this. We cannot casually stray into harm's way. We must remain sober and vigilant, which means staying as far away from temptation as possible.

Sure enough, the young man in Proverbs walked straight into hazardous territory:

There a woman met him,
With the attire of a harlot, and a crafty heart.
She was loud and rebellious. (vv. 10–11)

"Loud and rebellious" is not a description of this woman's personality. It's a personification of the spirit of lust, which is brash and defiant. It was that way in Solomon's day, and it's that way in modern times too. The spirit of lust makes itself known as loudly as possible and always pokes fun at sexual purity. Just look at today's movies and TV shows and see how the word *virgin* is mocked or how marriage is falsely and repeatedly shown as stifling and quarrelsome. That's the "loud and rebellious" spirit of lust at work. Sexual immorality is brazenly glorified, while innocence and fidelity are openly scorned.

The passage goes on to describe the woman as wandering about, "lurking at every corner" (v. 12). This is also how the spirit of lust operates today. Immorality is showcased everywhere, and it's the huge iceberg under the waterline of the Internet. A glut of movies, TV shows, magazines, and popular songs features it. A man will even find it difficult to drive down the block without seeing a salacious billboard or two.

Verse 13 says that the woman "caught" the young man and "kissed him." This was seen as brazen behavior back then, and it would be brazen behavior today too. And yet, strangely enough, this characteristic action of the spirit of lust can actually help us. The spirit of lust likes to shock us, but we can let that initial shock act as a warning. Whenever we feel the shock, we need to turn and run. The shock is a sign from God that we are in the wrong place and need to leave—immediately! In fact, if ever we *stop* being shocked by immoral behavior, then we're really in trouble.

After kissing the young man, the brazen woman made a surprising statement:

I have peace offerings with me;
Today I have paid my vows.
So I came out to meet you,
Diligently to seek your face,
And I have found you. (vv. 14–15)

The reference to "peace offerings" means she was a religious woman, active in the temple system. The modern equivalent of her statement would be, "I went to church today. Now that that's behind us, we can go have a little fun."

Here Solomon is giving us a glimpse of a person who pushes the boundaries of grace. She's saying, "Look: we can go sin, and afterward we'll repent, and everything will be okay." This type of behavior is not unusual in the church today. We know sin is wrong, yet still we engage in sin with the idea that we'll take care of it later.

Once I spoke with a man who was having an affair. I pleaded with him to end it, but he refused. In his rationalization he said, "I know what we're doing is wrong. But she and I are praying about it. In fact, we even pray together about it."

"That's the height of deception," I told him. "God always welcomes sinners home. Yet you are flagrantly and repeatedly entering the Holy of Holies with a woman with whom you are committing adultery. God will not be mocked."

The apostle Paul confronted this mind-set in Romans 6:1–2 when he asked, "What shall we say then? Shall we continue in sin that grace may abound? Certainly not!" Notice the emphasis at the end of that sentence. We can almost hear the disdain in the apostle's voice. He's snorting through his nose. He's pounding his fist on the table. Should we push the boundaries of God's grace? "Certainly not!"

Back in Proverbs 7:16–18, the immoral woman continued her seduction by cooing to the young man:

I have spread my bed with tapestry,
Colored coverings of Egyptian linen.
I have perfumed my bed
With myrrh, aloes, and cinnamon.
Come, let us take our fill of love until morning;
Let us delight ourselves with love.

Notice how she painted an enticing picture of the immorality to come. This is typical of how the spirit of lust acts. Immorality looks good on the outside. We're promised adventure and fun, fulfillment, relief, and respect. But the spirit of lust is always a liar! It entraps and ensnares. It ruins individuals and destroys families. The world refers to sexual immorality as "making love." But there is no real love in it, only deception and despair. Real lovemaking does not happen in a one-night stand. Real lovemaking involves rejoicing in the person you married through your entire lives together.

The immoral woman outlined her plan in Proverbs 7:18–20:

Come, let us take our fill of love until morning;
Let us delight ourselves with love.
For my husband is not at home;
He has gone on a long journey;
He has taken a bag of money with him,
And will come home on the appointed day.

"You won't get caught," she was saying. "Everything is taken care of." That's always the promise that the spirit of lust makes—a promise of secrecy, anonymity, and no consequences. And it's always a lie. Does anyone really believe he'll be the first person in human history to engage in immoral behavior and not suffer any consequences?

Here are two simple facts we can never forget. Mark them well:

1. God is always aware of all of our actions (Psalm 139).
2. Sin always has consequences (Galatians 6:7–8).

We glimpse some of those consequences of sin in Proverbs 7:21–23:

> *With her enticing speech she caused him to yield,*
> *With her flattering lips she seduced him.*
> *Immediately he went after her, as an ox goes to the slaughter,*
> *Or as a fool to the correction of the stocks,*
> *Till an arrow struck his liver.*
> *As a bird hastens to the snare,*
> *He did not know it would cost his life.*

We are not told the exact penalty for sin the young man received. He may have been plagued with a literal infection of the liver, and he may have literally died. Or the description may be metaphoric—perhaps he simply grew sick with sin and was found spiritually dead. Either way, the consequences were not pleasant. And that's the straightforward counsel: immorality always produces unpleasant consequences eventually.

In verses 24–26, Solomon offered another strong warning:

> *Listen to me, my children . . .*
> *Do not let your heart turn aside to her ways,*
> *Do not stray into her paths;*
> *For she has cast down many wounded,*
> *And all who were slain by her were strong men.*

That last warning never ceases to amaze me. *All* who were slain by her were strong men. Repeat: *all were strong men.* These were not folks with an initial penchant for immorality. They were leaders. People of strength and character. Upstanding. Upright. They believed they were above reproach. Yet still they fell.

Finally, the last verse in this passage should stop us all cold:

> *Her house is the way to hell,*
> *Descending to the chambers of death.* (v. 27)

The Bible says that repentance is available for all people, no matter what a person has done (Revelation 22:17). At the same time portions of Scripture do indicate that adulterers and fornicators go to hell. (See, for example, 1 Corinthians 6:9–10, which says that "neither fornicators . . . nor adulterers . . . will inherit the kingdom of God.")

What I believe these scriptures indicate is that the blood of Jesus covers all our sins, yet believers can still be in bondage. If a person is in open rebellion, however, and continues in a specific sin without regard to God's Word or the consequences of his or her sin, then that person should double-check whether he or she has truly come to Christ for repentance and salvation. Perhaps the professed believer was never saved in the first place. That in itself should cause us all to be wary of repeated sin (2 Corinthians 13:5).

As mentioned at the beginning of the chapter, the temptation to lust is huge today. The statistics of pornography usage are staggering. The divorce rates are overwhelming. I believe lust is one of the greatest threats to the church. Immorality is rampant in our culture, our pews, and even our pulpits.

But there is hope.

Even though the lust of the flesh is one of the most difficult spirits to overcome, the Bible gives clear guidance and shows the way out. Let's examine three reasons lust is so difficult to overcome and ways the Bible points to deliverance within that difficulty.

#1: Lust Springs from Natural Desires

The word *lust* actually means desire, and many translations interchange the two. In Greek, the word is *epithumeo*. It's a neutral word, meaning that the feeling can go either way, depending on which way it's directed.[1]

Notice Luke 22:15, where Jesus said to His disciples, "With fervent *desire* I have desired to eat this Passover with you before I suffer." That same word could have been translated as *lust*. Let me be clear that Jesus did not have evil lust. He simply had an *eager desire* to observe the Passover with His friends.

The neutrality of this word is a reminder that God gave us healthy and natural desires, including sexual desires. They are neither good nor bad in themselves, yet these desires can be fulfilled either in a godly or an ungodly way.

Ungodly desire, especially ungodly sexual desire, is what we call lust. Part of Satan's strategy is to turn our pure desires into evil ones and our ordinary fleshly desires into sinful lusts of the flesh. If we let him do that, we can easily slip into bondage to a spirit of lust.

Galatians 5:16–17 suggests a way to avoid that. Paul tells us to "walk in the Spirit, and [we] shall not fulfill the lust of the flesh. For the flesh lusts against the Spirit, and the Spirit against the flesh; and these are contrary to one another, so that you do not do the things that you wish."

The Spirit mentioned in this verse is the Holy Spirit. Notice that evil lust goes against the Spirit's wishes and that if we walk in close communion with the Holy Spirit, we will not succumb to lust. Notice also how we tend to look at the last part of that verse ("so that you do not do the things that you wish") in a negative light only. But it can be seen in a positive way too. We can be so in love with Jesus and so desire what God wants that we don't do the other things. We can be subject to the Spirit instead of to the flesh.

Romans 8:5–6 elaborates on this idea by pointing out that "those who live according to the flesh set their minds on the things of the flesh, but those who live according to the Spirit, the things of the Spirit. For to be carnally minded is death, but to be spiritually minded is life and peace." A big part of avoiding lust, in other words, involves what we allow our minds to dwell on. We need to deliberately set our minds on the things of the Holy Spirit. We'll talk about this in depth in the following chapter.

Romans 13:14 is also helpful in this context: "Put on the Lord Jesus Christ, and make no provision for the flesh, to fulfill its lusts." This reiterates the fact that *desire* is a neutral word. We can have either good desires or bad desires (lusts), and following our fleshly desires will lead us into dangerous areas. But if we purposely "put on the Lord Jesus Christ," meaning we consciously and deliberately see ourselves as "wearing Jesus" or "belonging to Jesus" or "surrounded by Jesus" then we will make no provision for those fleshly desires and will be able to focus instead on godly desires. This was a scripture I memorized when I was actively battling lust.

#2: Lust Is Always Deceptive

Lust is a lying spirit. It promises benefit but brings only heartache. It promises value but brings only destruction. Lust cannot be trusted. It must not be listened to or yielded to.

Read carefully the warning given in Proverbs 6:23–29. Again, the warning is geared specifically toward men, but the principles apply to both genders:

> For the commandment is a lamp,
> And the law a light;
> Reproofs of instruction are the way of life,
> To keep you from the evil woman,
> From the flattering tongue of a seductress.
> Do not lust after her beauty in your heart,
> Nor let her allure you with her eyelids.
> For by means of a harlot
> A man is reduced to a crust of bread;
> And an adulteress will prey upon his precious life.

Can a man take fire to his bosom,
And his clothes not be burned?
Can one walk on hot coals,
And his feet not be seared?
So is he who goes in to his neighbor's wife;
Whoever touches her shall not be innocent.

The theme of this passage is clear: Do we think we can actually commit immorality and not be harmed? Verse 26 describes this harm vividly, suggesting that succumbing to lust reduces a person to a "crust of bread." Think of the characteristics of a crust of bread. Dry. Stale. Forgotten. Overlooked. Not valued. Worthless except for feeding to ducks at a pond. That's the result of lust. And the passage goes on to suggest that if we give in to it, whatever we value will be destroyed and burned as if in fire.

The next three verses of Proverbs 6 are also valuable to this discussion:

People do not despise a thief
If he steals to satisfy himself when he is starving.
Yet when he is found, he must restore sevenfold;
He may have to give up all the substance of his house.
Whoever commits adultery with a woman lacks understanding;
He who does so destroys his own soul. (vv. 30–32)

The suggestion here is that people might excuse theft because hunger can be satisfied. But people won't excuse the actions of lust because lust can't be satisfied.

That's the deception of this spirit at work. Lust always promises satisfaction, but it never truly satisfies anyone. It leaves you wanting more. In a godly, pure marriage relationship, a person can be satisfied, but not so in an illicit affair. Only real love satisfies. A person who watches pornography always wants more. Those involved in an affair find the cravings only get worse as the participants go deeper into bondage.

If you've read my other books or know me from listening to my sermons at Gateway, it's no secret that I've lived a marred life. I'm able to speak about the deception of lust firsthand because in my earlier days I succumbed to an extramarital affair. By God's grace I repented and was led through a full restoration process by a team of godly leaders. I can tell you firsthand that my sin never satisfied me. For a season I lived a horrible, rotten, lonely, fearful, and defeated life. Praise God, He forgave me and delivered me fully. Praise the Lord that my wife forgave me, too, and I am fully restored to her. I can honestly say that my life today is filled with joy, peace, purity, and victory.

Let me add as a sidelight that nobody needs to experience an affair firsthand to know how horrible it is. If ever I give the impression that God can use a person more if he or she has had a bad past, then the Lord rebuke me, for that's a deceit in itself.

God hasn't used me *because of* my bad past. He's used me *in spite of* it. My sinful past hasn't helped me in any way; it has only hindered me. All the years that I walked in sin, fear, and shame were lost on my family and friends because I was so emotionally disconnected from them.

One time Debbie worried that she didn't have as powerful a testimony as me because she had never succumbed to evil as I had. She was saved at an early age and never strayed from the path of righteousness. When she told me this fear, I nearly wept. "Honey," I said, "your testimony is that God spared you from many things. I would do anything to be able to change positions with you."

I've since learned that feelings like Debbie's are common. Once, I said to my daughter when she was younger, "Stay with the Lord, and you will do greater things than I have ever done."

She said, "If I want God to use me more than He has used you, then I'll need to do a lot more bad things."

That broke my heart. I clarified to her—and I'll clarify to anyone who believes the same—that you do not need to have a bad story first to have a good story later. A testimony is not about how bad you were. It's about how good God is!

This brings us to our third point about why lust is such a difficult issue to overcome.

#3: *Lust Leads to Death*

Death is always the end result of succumbing to lust. It's the final, inevitable destination of a life given over to lustful desires.

Sometimes the death is physical, meaning a person actually loses his life. In an earlier chapter I mentioned someone I knew who had a heart attack while involved in an illicit affair. More often, the death is spiritual, meaning a person's sin eventually drives a wedge into his or her relationship with God. Spiritual passion and hunger diminish and eventually disappear. Desire for God wanes. A person's spiritual life becomes like that crust of bread—old, dry, and stale. Instead of desiring good things, that person craves only harmful things.

A lifestyle of lust can result in other deaths as well.

A marriage can die.

A business can die.

A career can die.

Opportunities for advancement can die.

Relationships with children can die.

Self-respect can die.

Inner peace can die.

Finances can die.

Health can die.

Joy can die.

Friendships can die.

The spirit of lust steals from people, kills them, and destroys them. A person consumed with lust cannot have a mind that's full of godly things so it can be creative and innovative and forward thinking. A mind filled with lust only wants one thing—a satisfaction it can never have.

James 1:14–15 says, "But each one is tempted when he is drawn away by his own desires and enticed. Then, when desire has conceived, it gives birth to sin; and sin, when it is full-grown, *brings forth death*." The word *desire* in this passage is that same Greek word *epithumeo* we looked at earlier in this chapter, the one that can also be translated as "lust." The verse could read: "Each one is tempted when he is drawn away by his own *lust* and enticed. Then, when *lust* has conceived, it gives birth to sin; and sin, when it is full-grown, brings forth death."

Romans 8:13 offers a similar strong warning. "For if you live according to the flesh you will die; but if by the Spirit you put to death the deeds of the body, you will live."

Love always brings life, and lust always brings death.

Eventually, that is.

Death is the final destination, the logical result. It's what will happen if we continue to give in to a life of lust, and the longer we remain involved with lustful activities, the stronger the pull toward death becomes.

But there is a way out.

I'm here to tell you that. It's not easy—far from it—but it is possible to move away from this death-dealing, often demonic way of life.

We can repent, confess, and seek accountability. We can pray for deliverance. We can seek help. And we can trust that God will provide us a way of escape.

First Corinthians 10:13 lays it out for us: "No temptation has overtaken you except such as is common to man; but God is faithful, who will not allow you to be tempted beyond what you are able, but with the temptation will also make the way of escape, that you may be able to bear it."

That means an escape route is always possible. God always offers deliverance. None of us need to be trapped by sin.

Once I was on a ski retreat with some of the leaders from our church. One of the elders was planning to ride the ski lift with me. But he fell right before he got on the lift and was delayed, so a woman I'd never met before climbed on the lift with me instead.

Right away I could tell in my spirit that something was wrong. We talked for a few minutes about simple matters; then she brazenly asked, "You want to come back to my room?" (Remember how the spirit of lust is loud, defiant, and shocking.)

"I'm married," I said quickly.

"So am I," she responded.

"Yeah," I said. My gloves were off now, and I was ready for spiritual battle. "But I'm married to both a man and a woman."

She gave me a surprised look. Before she could say anything, I continued, "I'm married to a wonderful woman named Debbie. And I've committed the rest of my life to a great man named Jesus Christ."

Now, when you're on a chairlift, you're high up in the air. You can't just hop off and go your own way. I had a captive audience. For the rest of our ride up the mountain, I told that woman all about Jesus!

God will make available a way of escape with every temptation we face. Our responsibility is to do our part in prayer. We are to ask God to lead us out of temptation and deliver us from evil. Then, with God's help, our responsibility is to utilize the escape route.

Do whatever is necessary to avoid evil. Turn off that computer. Get a filter installed. Change channels. Use a feature phone instead of a smartphone. Drive the other direction. Shut down your Facebook account. Change jobs. Sell your house and move to another city. Flee! Run!

I repeat: do whatever is necessary to avoid evil.

The Incredible Compassion of Christ

As mentioned earlier in this book, discipleship and deliverance go hand in hand. If we believe we're in bondage, then discipleship—learning more about Christ and learning to walk in His ways—will retrain the way we think, and deliverance will free us from spiritual bondage.

Some churches believe we need only one or the other, but both discipleship and deliverance are needed in the process. There are some who try to discipline the flesh while refusing to recognize the spiritual oppression. Others want to cast out demons but never instruct people in the faith. You can't cast out the flesh. And you can't disciple a demon. People need to be wary of evil but also grow in the grace and knowledge of Christ.

Second Corinthians 10:3–5 shows how deliverance and discipleship work together:

> For though we walk in the flesh, we do not war according to the flesh. For the weapons of our warfare are not carnal but mighty in God for pulling down strongholds, casting down arguments and every high thing that exalts itself against the knowledge of God, bringing every thought into captivity to the obedience of Christ.

That means we war in the spiritual realms, and we also need to grow in faith. We need both deliverance and discipleship.

The word *stronghold* used in that passage is a neutral word, just as *desire* is neutral. A stronghold can be either good or bad. Here's how it works in a harmful sense. You get tired or have a bad day at work, or business starts going down, or you have a disagreement with your spouse. You're weary or sad or worried, and you're tempted to run to the wrong stronghold.

Know what that usually is? It's a train of thought. Our minds are like Grand Central Station. Trains of thought pull in and out every second. Our destinations depend on which trains we board. The enemy will put a train of lustful thought in our minds. That's a train headed toward death—death of our marriages, death of our families, death of our careers, maybe even physical death. The more we board those harmful trains, the easier it becomes to ride them whenever we're stressed.

Here's a simple warning: Don't get on that train. Instead, board one that takes you to the stronghold of God.

Did you know God can be a stronghold? He's a fortress we can run to (or ride the train to) and be safe. In Him is life.

Philippians 4:8 says, "Whatever things are true, whatever things are noble, whatever things are just, whatever things are pure, whatever things are lovely, whatever things are of good report, if there is any virtue and if there is anything praiseworthy—meditate on these things." That's a verse to memorize and say to yourself each morning and evening, and whenever you're tempted to board the wrong train.

Let's pray right now.

Lord Jesus, Son of God, almighty God, we pray for Your help in this area of lust, this area that so many people struggle in. We repent of this sin. We confess that we have thought the wrong things and acted the wrong ways. We have boarded the wrong trains that lead to the destination of death. Father, we humble ourselves under Your righteous and mighty hand, asking that You would lift us up.

Deliver us from all spiritual oppression in this area. Free us from the spirit of lust. With the help of Your Holy Spirit, we will turn from evil and take on the fullness of Christ. Clothe us with Yourself, O Lord Jesus. Clothe us with Your compassion and kindness.

Let us fill our minds with the things of God. By Your grace, we will meditate on things that are righteous and pure and holy and true. We will board the right train to the right destination—the freedom and life You give us in Christ. You are our stronghold and deliverer. We worship You, almighty God. Amen.

If you've struggled with lust, I want you to know that there is great hope for you. When you repent, Jesus doesn't turn His back on you. He doesn't condemn you or shame you. He always welcomes you with arms open wide.

One of the NFL players who goes to our church started a Bible study, and one of the other professional athletes who came to the study confessed to the group that he'd been unfaithful years ago. The group encouraged him to confess to his wife, and he did. Do you know what his wife's response was? She said, "Babe, I'm deeply grieved by your sin. But Jesus forgives you, and so do I. In fact, I'm so sorry that you've carried this burden by yourself all these years."

That's a picture of the compassion that only Jesus can give us.

It feels as though we've covered much ground already, but we're only half finished with this subject. When it comes to lust, dealing with our actions is only one area of the battle. One of the greatest areas of struggle involves our minds. We'll cover this more in depth in the chapter to come.

Questions for Contemplation or Group Discussion

1. What stood out to you most from Proverbs 7?
2. Read Proverbs 10:24 and Luke 22:15. Then read Titus 2:12 and 2 Timothy 2:22. How can we know the difference between healthy, God-given desire and lust, which is a twisted desire?
3. Many people have been tempted with thoughts of dissatisfaction with God's provision in one or many areas of their lives—marriage, work, finances, friendships, and so on. How have you learned to take those thoughts captive and choose contentment?
4. Read Romans 8:13. According to this verse, what is the key to overcoming the lust of the flesh? How does the Holy Spirit help us?
5. Talk about the "compassion that only Jesus can give us." How have you experienced this in your own life?

Chapter Eight

BREAKING THE SNARES
IN YOUR MIND[1]

Take every thought captive to obey Christ.

—2 Corinthians 10:5 esv

A woman came to her small group leader and asked for help. She had been overeating recently and wanted to be held accountable in this area. She also described feeling angry much more than usual and found that she was snapping at her husband and children. This was creating problems in the home.

As the two talked, the root issues came out. Two months earlier the woman's husband had been laid off from work, and the woman was struggling with fear over the family's new, unsettled financial position as well as anger toward the past employer.

Every time this woman's life felt out of control, fear and anger welled up within her, she became irritable in spirit, and she turned to food as an emotional crutch. She knew she should be turning to God instead, asking to be filled with the fruits of the Holy Spirit. Yet she often found her flesh winning the battle. On impulse, she would sprint to the fridge or lash out in anger.

The woman and the counselor talked about forgiveness and how to handle anger biblically. They created a discipleship plan plus a new eating strategy and agreed to meet the following week for accountability.

The next time they saw each other, the leader asked the woman how she was doing. She said she hadn't departed from the plan. "But I've still got a problem with what's inside my mind," she added woefully, and here she tapped her forehead. "Every time this week that my life felt chaotic, I still found myself mentally rehearsing angry conversations I wanted to have with my husband's boss. The rage is still there. And I still found myself fighting the impulse to turn to food for comfort."

She's not alone. The devil and his bunch can play havoc with our thought lives. A person can be troubled by angry thoughts, suicidal thoughts, prideful thoughts, rebellious thoughts, or sexually illicit thoughts. A person can think wrong thoughts about abilities he or she has (or doesn't have) or be led into doubt or fear or constant anxiety. A person's mind can be muddled with confusion. He or she can be despondent for no reason or falsely filled with guilt.

Christian scholars debate exactly how demons are able to influence our thoughts. Some scholars insist that demons cannot interject harmful thoughts directly into our minds. Others insist that they can. Regardless, the question of how a demonic thought gets inside our heads is not the main issue to be concerned about. What matters is the fact that a harmful thought is present.

Ask yourself a simple question. If a thought is in your brain and it doesn't align with the righteous character of God, then with whom else does that thought align? There is no middle ground when it comes to our thought lives. The Bible describes Satan as "the father of lies" (John 8:44 NIV), and he wants to inject his deception into our heads any way he can.

We need to become free from all mental bondage. We need to make sure our thoughts are truly in line with Christ's.

But how?

The Mind Is a Battlefield

Jesus didn't die on the cross simply to give us eternal life. He also died on the cross to provide us with victorious lives. Salvation and victorious living go hand in hand. Yet even though we're forgiven and redeemed, saved, and on our way to heaven, we can still live a life of mental bondage. We're only as free as our minds are.

In Genesis 3:1 we find the origins of this bondage. Satan didn't take Eve captive with a gun, a bomb, a knife, or any obvious weapon. He did it with a simple question: "Has God indeed said . . . ?"

Do you see the tactic used? Before the devil can defeat anyone, he must try to disarm that person first. And the way he disarms us is by causing us to question what God has clearly said.

God had already told Adam and Eve what they needed to know. He had given them His word, clear boundaries for following Him and living righteously. Then Satan showed up, and he spoke three little words that caused Eve (and later Adam) to doubt God.

Satan has been using the same tactic ever since. But the good news is that Jesus triumphs over Satan; he can't win. Jesus came to earth as the incarnate Word of God, and through His work on the cross, He removed the curse from us. He also came to set our minds free. He said it directly in John 8:32: "You shall know the truth, and the truth shall make you free."

The war has been won. But battles still rage, and the battle of the mind is one of the fiercest. Second Corinthians 10:3–5 paints a powerful picture of the fighting:

> For though we walk in the flesh, we are not waging war according to the flesh. For the weapons of our warfare are not of the flesh but have divine power to destroy strongholds. We destroy arguments and every lofty opinion raised against the knowledge of God, and take every thought captive to obey Christ. (ESV)

The battle Paul described here is a spiritual and mental one, and the weapons at our disposal aren't natural weapons. They're supernatural weapons that have the God-given power to destroy demonic strongholds. And we're expected to use them.

Here's the battle plan as outlined in this passage. We destroy harmful arguments. We smash every high-sounding opinion that comes against what God has already spoken. And we do our best to take every illicit thought captive.

The Greek word translated "take captive" in this passage, *aichmalotizo*, comes from a root word that means "spear."[2] The imagery is that we can have victorious minds where every thought from the enemy that flits by is pressed up against a wall by the end of a spear and made to submit to Christ. No rogue thoughts are allowed to roam free in our minds. If we spot an inappropriate thought, then we don't entertain it. We attack it with a spear point. We make it "obey Christ."

The Greek word for "obey" is *hupakouo*, which means "to obey on the basis of having paid attention to."[3] In other words, we make every thought pay attention, or listen, to what Jesus has said.

That's exactly what Jesus did when Satan tempted Him in the wilderness. Satan attacked Jesus using words, empty promises, and tempting suggestions. But instead of succumbing to the temptation, Jesus responded by taking every one of Satan's ideas captive. Repeatedly He responded to Satan by pointing to Scripture and quoting it, saying, "It is written . . ." "It is written . . ." "It is written." Every temptation was countered by the revealed Word of God. Jesus took every one of Satan's suggestions captive by spear point. That's the model of living a free life.

The Bible teaches us that we cannot solve spiritual problems simply by using our willpower or our flesh. If we try to use these tools to overcome a harmful thought life, then we're fighting with the wrong weapons, and we're going to lose. If we want to become truly free, then we must make Jesus the Lord of our minds. We need to confess that our thoughts haven't been God-honoring. By prayer in the name of Jesus Christ, we must be delivered from demonic oppression. And then we must renew our minds by immersing our thoughts in Scripture.

The Holy Spirit will do the work here. He will renew us. But we must agree with what He's doing and cooperate. We must open the Bible. We must read and reread the text.

James 4:7 says, "Submit to God. Resist the devil and he will flee from you." If we don't submit to God first, then we don't have a chance of defeating the devil. Once we submit to God, however, and once we agree to cooperate with the Holy Spirit as He works in our lives, then we'll have the power to defeat the enemy. We must make a conscious mental decision that Jesus Christ will be honored by every thought that stays in our minds.

Thoughts might flit into our heads from a thousand different sources—what we read, what we watch, what people say, old memories that crop up, a billboard we pass by on the street. When these thoughts align with God's righteous character, we can choose to give focused and concentrated attention to them. If they do not align with God's character, the best strategy is to take them captive. Rather than entertaining such thoughts, we make them listen to God's Word. Then we reject them by consciously replacing them with Scripture.

The Bible is clear that our minds are battlefields. We must wage war to win the battle for our thought lives. So let's take a closer look at three ways we can fight successfully to become truly free in our minds.

Battle Strategy #1: Renewing Our Minds by Memorizing Scripture

When I was young and newly saved, I had a lot of problems with my thought life. Old memories and images kept replaying themselves in my mind, and it was easy to want to entertain those thoughts. I'd heard how Scripture memorization was a fundamental weapon for mental warfare, so I was eager to try it.

Too eager, it turned out. I attempted to memorize all of Psalm 119, the longest psalm in the Bible. I got as far as verse 9 and didn't get any farther. But even those nine verses helped.

I learned that my brain was like a hard drive on a computer, and for too many years I had programmed the wrong things on it. I was thinking defeated thoughts. I believed God would never want to use someone as messed up as I was. I was mired in anxiety, held under by false guilt. I'd been redeemed by Jesus and declared spotless in His presence, but I believed I was still covered in dirt. And the problem was that whenever I went to pull up something in my mind, my mind could only pull up what I'd programmed it to think.

So I started to memorize scripture. Not big chunks of it, as I had tried with Psalm 119, just specific verses related to the issues I was working through. I began to read my Bible every day too. Sure, there were days when I missed reading Scripture. There were also times I forgot Bible verses I thought I'd memorized. But as with anything else in life worth doing, the more I did it, the more proficient I became.

Gradually my mind began to change. Whenever I was tempted to think harmful thoughts, I'd pull up the newly saved documents on my "hard drive," the mental documents that contained God's Word. If ever I was tempted to think of myself as ruined, I pulled up what God's Word said about the hope and future that God was giving me. Gradually, I was learning what Paul meant when He said, "Do not be conformed to this world, but be transformed by the renewal of your mind" (Romans 12:2 ESV). Verse by verse, my thought life was being renewed.

These days, if I don't read my Bible each day, I feel a genuine sense that I'm missing something. I don't need to remind myself to do it anymore. The pattern is just ingrained in my life. I have a Bible on my phone, too, so it's far easier now just to pull up some scripture wherever I am—at the doctor's office, waiting for an appointment, or whatever.

The pattern Scripture sets forth for us is to renew our minds. That's what Scripture does for us.

Battle Strategy #2: Using God's Word as a Spiritual Weapon

The Word of God is one of the most powerful spiritual weapons at our disposal in the battle for our minds. Scripture is more powerful than we can fully understand. Ephesians 6:10–18 describes in detail the spiritual fight we're in and outlines God's provision for our protection:

> Finally, my brethren, be strong in the Lord and in the power of His might. Put on the whole armor of God, that you may be able to stand against the wiles of the devil. For we do not wrestle against flesh and blood, but against principalities, against powers, against the rulers of the darkness of this age, against spiritual hosts of wickedness in the heavenly places. Therefore take up the whole armor of God, that you may be able to withstand in the evil day, and having done all, to stand.
>
> Stand therefore, having girded your waist with truth, having put on the breastplate of righteousness, and having shod your feet with the preparation of the gospel of peace; above all, taking the shield of faith with which you will be able to quench all the fiery darts of the wicked one. And take the helmet of salvation, and the sword of the Spirit, which is the word of God; praying always with all prayer and supplication in the Spirit, being watchful to this end with all perseverance and supplication for all the saints.

Notice how Paul tells us to be strong in the Lord. He doesn't just order us to do it, but he tells us *how* to do it—in the Lord—and also how to prepare ourselves properly. He uses the analogy of a Roman soldier and describes six elements of his armor and how to use it correctly. We are instructed to put on the following:

- *The belt of truth.* A Roman soldier would "gird himself" with a wide belt to protect his "loins" (as some biblical translations say). The loin area of the body is used to reproduce and eliminate. When we're living according to God's Word, we reproduce truth and eliminate error. When we're not, we reproduce error and eliminate truth. The Bible says to use truth—the Word of God—as the basis of all reproduction and elimination. In other words, if something accords with the Word of God, we receive it and teach it to others, but if it clashes with the Word, we get rid of it.

- *The breastplate of righteousness.* A breastplate protected a soldier's vital organs, especially the heart. If an enemy soldier was looking for a kill shot, then he'd shoot for an unprotected heart. The devil always aims for the heart as well, seeking to rob us of our joy and faith. He shoots to kill by condemning us. He tells us that we're no good or that we've done too much wrong or that God loves other people more than He loves us. The breastplate of righteousness, however, declares that the blood of Jesus is the strongest cleansing and purifying agent in the universe. When our sin was touched by the blood of Christ, it was gone forever.

- *The helmet of salvation.* If an enemy slices off a man's head, the man is dead. The same is true for us. If our minds are destroyed, then we're as good as gone. Christ's salvation as outlined for us in the Bible protects our minds. Christ has saved us and made us "holy in his sight, without blemish and free from accusation" (Colossians 1:22 NIV). But again, I believe this verse reminds us to renew our minds with God's Word, to meditate on it and memorize it.

- *The shoes of the gospel of peace.* A Roman soldier's sandals had cleats on the bottom so he could stand solidly no matter what the terrain. That's what the gospel can do for us. Jesus came to make peace between us and a holy God. That means our lives are not about pleasing ourselves or making a ton of money or seeking fame or finding someone to love us. Our lives are about glorifying God. The devil wants us to take off our shoes so we'll be unstable when we walk. But living with constant reminders of the gospel of Christ keeps us steady. In the first chapter I told you about killing a rattlesnake on our property outside the city. Because of that, I always wear snakeproof boots. I think we need to wear the snakeproof boots of the gospel of peace every day!

- *The shield of faith.* A Roman soldier's shield was no small hubcap but a full-body shield. It was portable, strong, and protective. That's what faith is for us. How do we get faith? Faith comes from hearing the Word of God (Romans 10:17). That's why we need to constantly run scripture through our minds. The more we hear God's Word, the bigger and stronger our shield of faith becomes to block *all* the flaming arrows of the enemy!

- *The sword of the Spirit.* Hebrews 4:12 describes Scripture as "living and active, sharper than any two-edged sword" (ESV). We may read other books, but the Bible reads us. It is our only offensive weapon in the battle for our minds.

This is the full armor of God. It's more powerful than any other weapon at our disposal. Each day when we wake up, God wants us to dress for battle. He wants us wearing truth. He wants us wielding truth. He wants us living truth. And He wants us believing truth.

So again, the first way we can renew our minds is by memorizing scripture. The second way we can become free is by using the Word of God as a spiritual weapon. And the third way is by meditating on the Word.

Battle Strategy #3: Meditating on the Word of God

I've purposely made a distinction between *reading* scripture and *meditating* on scripture. The two go hand in hand, but they are not the same. I can read a newspaper or a car magazine, but I'm not meditating on what I read.

Meditating means we give focused and concentrated thought to something. We really think about it. We chew on something as a sheep chews its cud—again and again and again.

Have you ever seen a sheep do this? A sheep has only one stomach, but the stomach has four sections. When a sheep eats something, it swallows the food first, then regurgitates it and chews, swallows again, regurgitates again, chews, swallows, regurgitates, and so on until the food is fully digested.

A little gross, maybe, but that's basically what the word *meditate* means. It's a process of regurgitating and chewing on the words.

This is not the same as Eastern or New Age meditation, where we're told to empty our minds and think about nothing. Biblical meditation definitely involves thinking about something—scripture. It means we read scripture, then read it again. We put scripture into our hearts and recall it day in and day out.

When I memorize scripture, I memorize it a phrase at a time, a verse at a time. I memorize it by meditating on each phrase. I say the phrase, then repeat it, then repeat it again and again. All the time I'm mulling it. I'm asking myself questions, such as *What is this scripture saying to me?* or *What does this phrase tell me about God's character?* I think about that phrase or verse all day long and think of ways to apply it.

When I was in that emergency room in Australia, Debbie was not allowed to stay with me. I was losing a lot of blood, and several times the doctors mentioned the very real possibility of my death. As I lay there alone in the hospital gurney, harmful, fearful thoughts ran through my mind. I had the choice of entertaining those thoughts or battling them.

I knew my life was in God's hands, that He would never leave me nor forsake me (Hebrews 13:5) and that all my days were numbered by Him (Psalm 139:16). So I went to battle. One of the first things I did was phone my children to enlist prayer support. All my children are adults now, and all are walking with the Lord. They all live within about five miles of us, so they gathered at the house and prayed for me.

Then I lay back on my pillow and brought to mind all the Scripture verses I could remember. I started at the beginning of the Bible, in Genesis, and I walked through the Bible chapter by chapter, book by book, meditating on each one that came to mind. Then I recalled a snippet of Ezekiel 16:6 and remembered I had a Bible downloaded on my phone, so I looked up the verse just to make sure of the words. "When I passed by you and saw you struggling in your own blood, I said to you in your blood, 'Live!' Yes, I said to you in your blood, 'Live!'"

I knew God was talking specifically to the nation of Israel in that verse, but when I read it, a new and firm sense of peace washed over me. Within my spirit I sensed the Lord saying to me, *This is not your time, Robert. You're not going to die. I spoke this verse to the nation of Israel once, and I'm speaking it to you today: I see you struggling in your own blood, yet I'm saying, "Live!"*

Psalm 107:20 tells us that the Word of God is actually a healing agent. Yes, the Word of God does slash with a sword, as Hebrews 4:12 describes. But paradoxically the same sword that is so powerful in fighting battles can also heal. The Word of God finds our wounds and heals them like a surgeon's scalpel. Our task is not simply just the reading of Scripture but memorizing it and meditating on God's Word so it renews our minds.

One of my favorite Scripture passages is Psalm 1:1–3. It's such a powerful promise:

> *Blessed is the man*
> *Who walks not in the counsel of the ungodly,*
> > *Nor stands in the path of sinners,*
> > *Nor sits in the seat of the scornful;*
> *But his delight is in the law of the LORD,*
> > *And in His law he meditates day and night.*
> *He shall be like a tree*
> > *Planted by the rivers of water,*
> > *That brings forth its fruit in its season,*
> > *Whose leaf also shall not wither;*
> *And whatever he does shall prosper.*

The passage says that a person who doesn't walk in the counsel of the ungodly is blessed. But what might the counsel of the ungodly be? I believe it includes any thoughts that don't come from God or align with God's Word.

It's always a temptation to listen to the world's plan for living. The world insists we need to be rich, famous, and powerful. We need to drive all the right cars and wear all the right clothes and have snappy comebacks to anyone who gets in our way.

But Psalm 1 paints a different picture. It says we're blessed when we delight in God's Word and—get this—when we *meditate* on God's law day and night. What a promise this is! The Bible says that when we do this we'll be like trees planted by streams of water—never be at a loss for vitality and creativity and sustenance. We'll be like leaves that don't wither—stable in our freshness and forever blooming and whole, not withered, cracked, and dry.

Psalm 1 also says that a man who meditates on God's Word is guaranteed prosperity. Now, I know we need to be careful when we even mention the word *prosper* because it's been so misused by churches and ministers in the past. But *prosper* is a biblical word. It's right there in Psalm 1:3, so it must have something important to say to us.

What does it mean to be told we're going to prosper? It's not a promise that we'll live in sensual indulgence or a have an abundance of material possessions. It means we will live as God intends us to live. We will bear abundant spiritual fruit (Galatians 5:22–23). Our activities and intentions will result in their divinely intended fulfillment (Philippians 1:6). We will live lives that are pleasing to almighty God (2 Corinthians 5:9). And that's only half of what it means for a Christian to prosper!

I used to think that meditating on the Word of God was too hard and that I couldn't do it. But when I actually began doing it, I came to see that it's the easiest thing in the world. And meditating on Scripture produces the deepest peace I've ever had.

To use the computer analogy again, a computer has both hardware and software. The hardware is the actual guts of the computer—the physical components that make everything run. The software is the programs that run on the hardware.

The human brain is our hardware. The thoughts that run through our minds are like software.

Ever since the fall in Genesis 3, our minds have been infected, like a computer program with a virus. This virus steals from us the knowledge of God and causes us to think and act in ways we were never designed to think and act. But the good news is that when we meditate on Scripture, we download the software that reprograms our brains to think and act properly. We can literally retrain our brains to think God thoughts, not corrupted thoughts.

Let's make this highly practical. When our thinking is skewed, it's best to go to the verses that specifically address whatever issue is plaguing our minds. Let's look at a few examples.

- *Fear.* "For God has not given us a spirit of fear, but of power and of love and of a sound mind" (2 Timothy 1:7).
- *Forgiveness.* "If we confess our sins, He is faithful and just to forgive us our sins and to cleanse us from all unrighteousness" (1 John 1:9).
- *Anxiety.* "Be anxious for nothing, but in everything by prayer and supplication, with thanksgiving, let your requests be made known to God; and the peace of God, which surpasses all understanding, will guard your hearts and minds through Christ Jesus" (Philippians 4:6–7).
- *Temptation.* "No temptation has overtaken you except such as is common to man; but God is faithful, who will not allow you to be tempted beyond what you are able, but with the temptation will also make the way of escape, that you may be able to bear it" (1 Corinthians 10:13).

- *Irritability.* "Rejoice always, pray without ceasing, in everything give thanks; for this is the will of God in Christ Jesus for you" (1 Thessalonians 5:16–18).
- *Lack of Self-Control.* "I appeal to you therefore, brothers, by the mercies of God, to present your bodies as a living sacrifice, holy and acceptable to God, which is your spiritual worship. Do not be conformed to this world, but be transformed by the renewal of your mind, that by testing you may discern what is the will of God, what is good and acceptable and perfect" (Romans 12:1–2 ESV).

When is the best time to meditate on scripture? Anytime, of course. But Deuteronomy 6:6–9 outlines four specific times when it's especially helpful:

> And these words which I command you today shall be in your heart. You shall teach them diligently to your children, and shall talk of them when you sit in your house, when you walk by the way, when you lie down, and when you rise up. You shall bind them as a sign on your hand, and they shall be as frontlets between your eyes. You shall write them on the doorposts of your house and on your gates.

The passage speaks specifically about teaching Scripture to children, but the times it mentions are also applicable to meditating on scripture. Those four times are . . .

- when we get up in the morning;
- when we go to bed at night;
- when we're sitting around the house, not doing anything; and
- when we're traveling somewhere.

Note that those are the four main times the devil is most prone to attack our minds. When we go to bed at night, for instance, it's easy to lie there in the dark and entertain harmful thoughts. Here comes the worry. Here comes the fear. Here comes the lust. Here come the anxiety and irritability.

When we have Scripture in our minds and hearts during such times, we are armed and dangerous. We can take every thought captive and defeat any harmful ones. If we don't have Scripture in our spirit at those times, though, we're vulnerable. Our willpower alone is not as powerful as the devil. He may be able to influence us and put us into bondage.

Fortunately God's Word is more powerful than the devil. It can defeat the devil's mental suggestions every time if we use it. The key is not that we *remove* the negative thought from our mind, but to *replace* it with a more powerful thought from God's Word.

If I'm lying in a hospital bed and I'm afraid, then it does me no good if I just say to myself, "Robert, stop thinking about fear." If I try that, fear immediately becomes the proverbial elephant in the room. I'm trying hard, trying hard, trying hard not to think about the elephant, which means I'm actually thinking about the elephant constantly. The key is that I must replace the thought of the elephant with a different, greater thought.

That's why we must have our scripture ready in our minds, particularly for these four vulnerable times of the day. If the devil comes against us with condemnation, then we know what to do. We come back with scripture!

The Ease of God's Deliverance

Marriage Today founder Jimmy Evans tells the story of a friend of his who is one of the most disciplined people he knows. The friend met with Jimmy one day and described how, despite his highly disciplined lifestyle, there was one area of his life he simply could not get under control. "I'm addicted to pornography," the friend said, "and I just can't conquer it. I don't know what to do. I've tried every single thing I know to get set free from this, and I'm at a loss." (We discussed this issue in depth in the last chapter, but big parts of this chapter apply to it as well.)

Jimmy prayed for the man, that God would deliver him from any spiritual oppression. Then, in five short minutes, Jimmy told the friend about the power of Scripture and what it meant to meditate on God's Word. Jimmy outlined the plan quickly and simply. "Get a specific scripture in your mind," he told the man. (For this problem, he recommended Philippians 4:8.) "Then every time the temptation to lust comes, deliberately bring that verse to mind and meditate on it."

The friend went home. A few days later he called Jimmy.

"I'm free," the friend said. "I'm 100 percent free. When I left your office that day I went home and I began to do exactly what you described. I haven't lost a battle yet. The devil still attacks me, but now I know what to do. I'm amazed at how simple it is."

I love that story, and I've witnessed firsthand many stories just like it. We can live our lives free from fear; free from anxiety; free from thoughts of suicide, low self-esteem, and condemnation; free from lust; free from addictions; and so much more. We just need to learn how to fight for our minds.

Let's pray right now.

Lord Jesus, we declare You Lord of our thought lives. We bring every thought captive to You, and we declare war in Jesus' name on any stronghold of the enemy in our lives. We dedicate ourselves to living according to Your Word. We gird our loins with truth. We put on the breastplate of righteousness, the helmet of salvation, and the shoes of the gospel of peace. We arm ourselves with the sword of the Spirit. We will be careful to never walk in the counsel of the wicked. We will delight in Your Word and meditate on it day and night.

In the name of Jesus Christ, we thank You for freedom. In the name of Jesus, we bind Satan and all his evil work. Holy Spirit of

God, we pray that You will come into our lives with Your full power and that You will fill us with the full measure of God.

In Jesus Christ's name we ask these things and pray, amen.

In this chapter we've talked about how to become free from mental bondage. In the next one we'll talk about emotional bondage, a similar struggle that can be at the root of how other problems manifest themselves in our lives. The good news is that Jesus came not only to free our minds but to heal our souls. We'll find out how that works in the pages ahead.

Questions for Contemplation or Group Discussion

1. Which part of this chapter was most helpful to you?
2. Read 2 Corinthians 10:3–5. What does it mean to take thoughts "captive" or "into captivity"? Why is this possible only with the help of the Holy Spirit?
3. Read Hebrews 4:12. What describes your background with the Bible, and what does this verse tell us about Scripture?
4. What are some of your favorite passages of Scripture that you've memorized?

Chapter Nine

BREAKING THE SNARES OF PAST WOUNDS

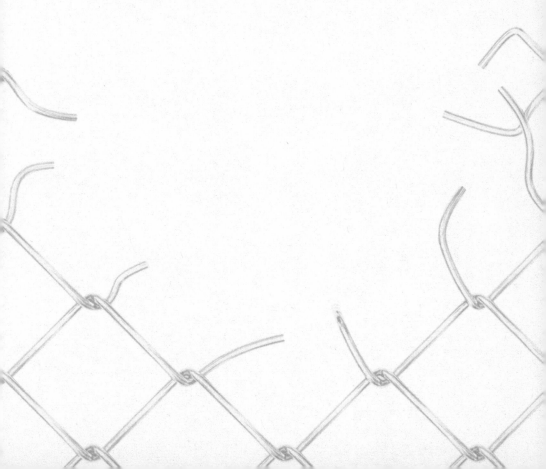

A bruised reed he will not break.

—ISAIAH 42:3 NIV

When I was just a boy, five or six years old, I had a problem pronouncing the letter *R*. If your name is John Smith, then that's not a problem. But if your name is Wobert Mowwis, then you're prime fodder to become the butt of playground jokes. Right about that time my family moved to a new city—Marshall, Texas— and I distinctly remember the kids at school laughing at me and calling me names.

I started going to speech therapy. In the long run the therapy would prove beneficial, but in the short term it added to the sense of different-ness I felt. Each day during coloring time I was singled out to leave the classroom so I could attend therapy, which only added to my hurt. I always wondered what I was missing during coloring time.

I've had a form of color blindness all my life. For years as a kid I thought this eye problem was caused by having to leave class in first grade during coloring time. Even after I grew up and knew better, the color blindness has posed a few problems. I've driven through flashing red lights while thinking they were yellow. Over time, however, the color blindness has emerged into more of a wardrobe issue.

These days Debbie picks out all my clothes. Once she was out of town on a women's retreat and forgot to lay out my clothes for the week-end services. I dressed myself, then came to church. A wife of one of our associate pastors took one look at me, shook her head, and said, "Debbie's out of town—right?"

Fortunately the speech therapy paid off for me as a boy, and my speech improved quite quickly. By the time second grade rolled around, you couldn't distinguish the way I talked from that of any other kid. I even learned to relish publish speaking. By the time I was twelve, I was doing ventriloquism shows.

My speech issue was completely healed. But those emotional wounds were still there—the feeling of being left out; the feeling that maybe I was missing something; the feeling of being unacceptably different. Those feelings stayed with me for years.

One of my staff members, Tommy Briggs, experienced a similar emotional wound while growing up. His father was a sharecropper, and the family grew up in poverty. To top it off, he had a speech impediment just as I did. He distinctly remembers the first book report he ever gave. It was on the book *Bambi*. Tommy got up in front of the class and mispronounced the title of the book. The class laughed.

Tommy carried that wound with him for many years. He always thought of himself as inferior to others—just the farm kid whose family didn't have enough money. His wounding held him back from doing things he wanted to do. It became a stronghold for the enemy, and it kept Tommy away from all the Lord had in store for him.

Fortunately the Lord got hold of Tommy's life and began to do a real work of healing in him. Tommy describes the healing as more of a gradual process than a onetime event. But it was definite and concrete.

Today Tommy is one of the leaders at our Kairos seminars—events we hold at our church that help people with emotional healing. At our last event, more than a thousand people attended. There was Tommy, up onstage, leading the entire group. He spoke clearly and confidently. Tommy has described to me a sense of emotional freedom he now feels when speaking in public. The Lord has done a remarkable work in his life, and the wounds of his childhood are gone.

Sadly, not everyone can say the same.

Wounds can hold us in bondage. These wounds tend to be deep within us, and we can't get over them by ignoring them. The issue is whether—and how—we allow the Lord to deal with the wound.

Jesus' Work

Luke 4:16–22 tells us that Jesus came to Nazareth, the town where He had been brought up. As was His custom, "He went into the synagogue on the Sabbath day, and stood up to read. And He was handed the book of the prophet Isaiah. And when He had opened the book" (vv. 16–17), He read:

> *"The Spirit of the LORD is upon Me,*
> *Because He has anointed Me*
> *To preach the gospel to the poor;*
> *He has sent Me to heal the brokenhearted,*
> *To proclaim liberty to the captives*
> *And recovery of sight to the blind,*
> *To set at liberty those who are oppressed;*
> *To proclaim the acceptable year of the LORD."* (vv. 18–19)

When Jesus had finished reading, all eyes were fixed on Him. This was a Messianic prophecy, and everybody in the synagogue knew it. They wondered what Jesus was about to say about the text. The words He spoke next were simple yet profound: "Today this Scripture is fulfilled in your hearing" (v. 21).

Let me paraphrase. Jesus was saying, "I'm *Him*. Your Messiah is here. And what I've just read—these five foundational ministries that Isaiah described—is what the Messiah will do."

What were those foundational ministries?

- *To preach the gospel and provide salvation.* Two phrases in that passage relate to this. Jesus came to "preach the gospel to the poor" and to "proclaim the acceptable year of the LORD." Jesus wanted all to know that His work on the cross would bridge the gap between a holy God and sinful mankind.

- *To model the work of Spirit baptism.* Jesus said, "The Spirit of the Lord is upon Me / Because He has anointed Me." We know the Holy Spirit had descended on Jesus when John baptized Him in the Jordan River (Luke 3:21–22). And Jesus would promise His church a powerful encounter with the Holy Spirit after His death and resurrection.
- *To heal people physically.* Jesus said He would provide "recovery of sight to the blind."
- *To deliver people from spiritual bondage.* Jesus said He would "proclaim liberty to the captives."
- *To provide emotional healing.* Jesus said He would "heal the brokenhearted" and "set at liberty those who are oppressed." The King James Version of the Bible translates this second phrase this way: "To set at liberty them that are bruised."

It's that last work—to provide emotional healing—that we want to look at in this chapter. Since I find the wording particularly helpful here, let's use the King James. Two parts exist to this work: Jesus heals the brokenhearted, and He sets at liberty those who are bruised. Let's look at both facets of this work together.

#1: Jesus Came to Heal Broken Hearts

In Greek this term "brokenhearted" is two words put together. The first word is *suntribo*, which means "to break in pieces" or "shatter."[1] It's what happens if a glass jar gets bumped off a counter and falls on the kitchen floor. The jar breaks into so many tiny shards that it's unrecoverable. The second word is *kardia* in Greek, which means "heart"[2]—it's where we get our English word *cardiac*.

Jesus was saying that He can do for our hearts what initially looks impossible. Imagine being able to repair that glass jar shard by splintered shard so that it looks completely whole again. Jesus does that for our shattered hearts.

Think about that term—*shattered*. Has your heart ever been broken? I mean really broken? Has your heart ever been so wounded it seemed absolutely irreparable? The good news is there's someone who can heal that. Jesus can put every piece back in place.

When I was in college, one of the students was known for being the campus clown. He was always making a joke of everything. Additionally, he led a rebellious and immoral lifestyle. The Lord placed this guy on my heart to pray for him. I shared with a few other students about the burden I felt, but they told me to forget it. The guy was too far gone, they insisted. He wasn't worth expending any effort on. They had tried to help him a few times, but nothing had ever come of it. Still the Lord kept bringing this guy to my mind. So I kept praying for him and then decided to become his friend. It wasn't easy, but it happened. We even became roommates. He began to trust me and finally opened up about his past.

It quickly became clear that his wild behavior as a college student stemmed from a deep emotional wounding he had experienced as a child. His father had left home the day he was born. Then his mother had died of cancer. He acted the way he did because his heart was shattered. But he was not too far gone. Jesus began to do a real work in him. Piece by piece, Jesus put his heart back together. Today that same guy is healed of his emotional wounds. He became a pastor and is helping others find forgiveness, grace, and healing through Jesus Christ.

Life is often difficult, and our hearts can become broken for a lot of reasons. Perhaps a parent disappointed us or hurt us when we were young. Perhaps we were jilted by a girlfriend or boyfriend during our teen or young adult years. Perhaps we didn't get a job we wanted, or we've never broken through to a certain level in our careers. Perhaps someone close to us has died, or someone we loved has spurned us. No matter what the specific reasons for our broken hearts, the root cause is usually the same—a great loss or disappointment. We feel hurt, scorned, forgotten, crushed, or rejected.

Even though we are blessed as Christians, Jesus never promises us a pain-free life (John 16:33). Sorrows and tribulations will come to us, and it's not wrong to grieve, lament, or feel loss. When His friend Lazarus died, Jesus responded by weeping (John 11:35). That's a natural and healthy response.

The Bible even shows us a healthy way to grieve—by showing us how *not* to do it. "I do not want you to be ignorant," Paul wrote in 1 Thessalonians 4:13, ". . . lest you sorrow as others who have no hope." By contrast, we are to sorrow as those who *do* have hope and also to comfort each other in our pain (v. 18).

Great problems can arise if we do not grieve in this biblical manner. If we let our hurts go untreated by Jesus, if we hold on to grudges or feelings of being rejected, if we see our hurts as untreatable, then these can all become footholds for the enemy to influence our lives. Untreated hurt and feelings of rejection can easily enslave a person and keep him or her in bondage.

Have you ever seen a person with a broken heart who has not been healed by Christ? Let me point out seven ways that an untreated wound can manifest itself.

Anger. Extreme or inappropriate displays of anger are often evidence of an emotional stronghold stemming from past pain. Some people attribute such outbursts of anger to a personality disorder, and sometimes this can be the case. Yet at other times the anger is due to a person being demonically influenced.

I got beat up many times as a youngster. It happened once too often, and something snapped in me. From then on a fight would trigger such a rage in me that I demonstrated an extremely high level of strength, perhaps even a supernatural strength. No one could beat me after that. And I hadn't done any great weight training or conditioning. I believe I was being unduly influenced by a spirit of rage.

The Bible points to the existence of such spirits. King Saul disobeyed God, and the Lord rejected Saul as king over Israel. In 1 Samuel 19:9, the Bible says that a "distressing spirit from the LORD came upon Saul." This particular spirit was a spirit of rage, and the fact that the Bible says it came from God is simply an indication that all demonic spirits are subject to God's sovereignty. One evening as Saul sat in his house with his spear in his hand, the young shepherd David played music on his harp. The spirit came upon Saul, and Saul threw his spear directly at David, intent upon pinning him to the wall. Fortunately David evaded the spear and escaped (v. 10). When people exhibit great anger like that—to the extent they try to physically harm other people—it could be the work of an evil spirit.

Insecurity. Constantly demanding attention, needing to be emotionally propped up on a regular basis, being overly concerned about appearance and position—all those can be signs of insecurity. Sometimes it's just a character quirk. But often people are insecure because they've been wounded deeply, the wound has been allowed to go untreated and fester, and the pain has become a foothold for the enemy to use.

Consider the security of Paul, who said, "I can do all things through Christ who strengthens me" (Philippians 4:13). A secure person is constantly aware of God's call upon his life and of the work Christ has done for him or her on the cross. Romans 8:14–15 says, "For as many as are led by the Spirit of God, these are [children] of God. For you did not receive the spirit of bondage again to fear, but you received the Spirit of adoption by whom we cry out, 'Abba, Father.'"

I encourage those who feel painfully insecure to soak themselves in this verse. Deliverance may be necessary.

Pride. Pride can manifest itself in different ways. Prideful people tend to talk a lot about their own accomplishments, portray themselves as better than anyone else, and look down on others. They may like to give their opinions on everything or dominate discussions. They may believe they are always right and everyone else is wrong. Or they may be the kind of individuals who stand apart from others and refuse to accept needed help. Some may even exhibit a reverse pride that enjoys being different and refuses to conform to expectations.

Sometimes pride is the result of deep wounding. The person has vowed never to be hurt again and may try to accomplish this by trying to know all or be all or do all. Some may seek prominent, powerful, or dominant positions or take inappropriate risks because they can't admit they're wrong. When such behavior becomes extreme, bondage to a spirit of pride may be involved. This person may need deliverance as well as discipleship.

Independence. By "independence" I'm talking about a person who says, "I don't need anyone. I can make it on my own." It's very difficult to develop a close or meaningful relationship with this kind of person because he or she constantly holds you at arm's length. Independent people tend to be very guarded and won't allow anyone to become close as a friend. They won't listen to counsel. They will do what they want no matter what.

This type of independence often stems from rejection or perceived abandonment in the past. As a safeguard against the pain, such people have erected walls around themselves, determined that no one will have the chance to reject them again. Too often this pain has become a foothold for the enemy to use, and independence becomes a stronghold.

Touchiness. Ever notice how you need to walk on eggshells when you're around some people? They are easily offended, and they take comments very personally. You can't joke around with them; you have to be extremely careful around them. You never know if they are holding a grudge over something you allegedly did or said or forgot to do or say.

Some people are naturally more sensitive to nuances of behavior than others, but that's not what we're talking about here. We're talking about wounded people who have become ultrasensitive to slights and vigilant about making sure that no one steps on their toes again. Somehow, the teaching of 1 Corinthians 13:5 is forgotten—that love "is not easily angered" (NIV). Being prickly, touchy, and quick to take offense are signs that a person has allowed a hurt to become a stronghold for the enemy.

Excessive Shyness or Loneliness. Again, I'm not talking about a personality quirk here. I'm talking about an overt fear of people. We've talked about this in other chapters. Early on in our marriage, if Debbie walked across the room to speak to someone, I would be left with a crippling fear and the feeling of abandonment, which resulted in anger against my wife.

A Need to Control. When a person is being harassed by the spirit of rejection, he or she can exhibit that influence by being either a petty dictator or a champion manipulator. The person will constantly seek to arrange others, put others in their place, or control their responses. The underlying motivation, of course, is to ensure that the controller is not hurt again. Often people become controllers because of a deep-seated fear that if they loosen their grip, their lives will spin out of control.

Control can have many faces. Some people who have the spirit of control can sometimes appear very charming—at least at first. Others can be overbearing—interrupting others and refusing to yield the floor to anyone who might want to do things differently. Controlling people tend to be poor listeners. Some try to control others through overt intimidation, while others will try to make you pity them or even resort to tears.

Anger, insecurity, pride, independence, touchiness, shyness, a need to control—any of these can be evidence of a broken heart—and signs that the enemy is at work. But Jesus' work is to heal the brokenhearted and set at liberty those who are bruised.

We've looked at what it means to be brokenhearted. Let's look at the second facet of Jesus' work now.

#2: *Jesus Came to Liberate the Bruised*

Several years ago I was ministering to a couple, and at first glance the two of them looked perfectly fine. But several "telling marks" had surfaced in their marriage and health, which is why they had come for counsel. As they sat in my office, the man dominated our conversation. He spent most of our time together bragging about how God was using him mightily in life. The woman just sat there dejectedly, saying nothing. She looked on the verge of tears.

As I sat there listening, God gave me an insight into the woman's life. Inside her soul the woman had black eyes, bloodied lips, and broken bones. She was being ignored. Overlooked. Rebuked. Shamed. Chastised for "cutting into the man's ministry time." Inwardly she was covered in bruises.

I stopped the husband midsentence and said, "Can't you see what's happening to your wife?"

The man shook his head.

I said, "You cannot claim to serve God while ignoring your family like this. You cannot go forward with the Lord until you get this right with your wife. Right now you should be on your knees, begging your wife's forgiveness for not cherishing her as Christ has called you to do. You need to stay by her side until she is healed."

A physical bruise is caused by inward bleeding. A person's skin is hit, and at first there is no outward sign. But the small capillaries under the skin have been injured, and soon a dark, discolored spot appears at the place of wounding.

Emotional bruising can follow the same course. A person suffers through rejection or loss or hurt, and at first there's no outward sign. But inwardly the person is bleeding, and soon the signs of that hurt will appear for anyone to see.

You may be in a relationship right now that's similar to what that woman who came to counseling with her husband went through. If your earthly husband won't sit at your feet until you're healed, you need to know that your heavenly Father will. Jesus washed the feet of His disciples. He will never leave you or forsake you.

Yet you have a responsibility in this too. You cannot let your inward bruising go untreated. It's not wrong to grieve if we've been hurt. But we must go to Jesus with our hurt to allow Him to heal us. Second Corinthians 1:3–5 offers us this promise of comfort:

> Blessed be the God and Father of our Lord Jesus Christ, the Father of mercies and God of all comfort, who comforts us in all our tribulation, that we may be able to comfort those who are in any trouble, with the comfort with which we ourselves are comforted by God. For as the sufferings of Christ abound in us, so our consolation also abounds through Christ.

An emotional bruise, when left untreated, can become an entry point to demonic activity. Often the real problem is a lack of forgiveness. A person has been hurt and is angry, but then the sun goes down on that anger, and the devil is given a foothold (Ephesians 4:26–27 NIV).

In Matthew 18, Peter asked Jesus, "How often shall my brother sin against me, and I forgive him?" (v. 21). Jesus answered, "Seventy times seven" (v. 22). Then Jesus told a story.

The servant owed a staggering amount of money—something like $52 million in today's currency—to his master. Unable to pay the debt, he went to the master, fell at his feet, and begged for leniency. Fortunately for the servant, the master had pity and wiped the debt clean. But then that same servant, feeling smug, went and found someone who owed him a trifling amount of money—about forty-four bucks—and threw this poor guy into debtor's prison until all could be repaid.

When the master found out about this, he grew extremely angry. Matthew 18:32–33 records his specific words. "You wicked servant! I forgave you all that debt because you begged me. Should you not also have had compassion on your fellow servant, just as I had pity on you?" And then, according to verse 34, the master "*delivered him to the torturers* until he should pay all that was due him."

Wow! That's extreme. I wonder, *Who exactly are those torturers?*

(Another version of the Bible calls them *tormenters.*) And then we read Jesus' words in the verse that follows: "So My heavenly Father also will do to you if each of you, from his heart, does not forgive his brother his trespasses" (v. 35).

Is Jesus really saying we will be tortured if we don't forgive? Some commentators explain His statement by saying simply that trouble will come upon a person if he doesn't forgive others. But I believe the verse holds forth a much stronger warning. In 1 Corinthians 5, Paul rebuked the church at Corinth for harboring in their midst a person who habitually did evil. Paul ordered them to "deliver such a one to Satan for the destruction of the flesh, that his spirit may be saved in the day of the Lord Jesus" (v. 5). In other words, Paul was telling the Corinthians to hand the person over to Satan.

Why would God's Word ever issue such a statement? This pattern of discipline had been established in the Old Testament. Many times when the nation of Israel sinned and didn't repent, God would turn His people over to their enemies. Why? God hoped they would repent. Discipline was always done in the hope that they would come back to God. The principle is straightforward—when people really know what bondage is like, they're apt to seek deliverance.

Back to the Matthew passage, I believe Jesus was essentially saying, "Look: if you're not going to forgive someone when you've been forgiven much, then you're going to go into bondage. You're going to be miserable until you repent, forgive, and are delivered. I don't want you to be miserable. I don't want you to be enslaved either. I want you to come back to God. The only reason this is happening is that you need to understand you can't be delivered until you repent."

Note another scripture that warns us how Satan can take advantage of us if we don't forgive. Paul wrote in 2 Corinthians 2:10–11, "Now whom you forgive anything, I also forgive. For if indeed I have forgiven anything, I have forgiven that one for your sakes in the presence of Christ, *lest Satan should take advantage of us; for we are not ignorant of his devices.*"

How can Satan take advantage of us when we don't forgive? In 2 Corinthians 11:14, Paul notes that "Satan himself transforms himself into an angel of light." Satan pretends to be a good angel, but he's not. That means that withholding forgiveness can feel falsely comforting to the injured person. Not forgiving can actually feel good. But that's always a counterfeit feeling. That's Satan holding up a mask and pretending he's a comforter. In the end, withholding forgiveness always ends up hurting us.

Let's say Debbie and I are in an argument, and I leave feeling bruised. Here's what Satan does. One of his bunch puts his arm around my shoulder and says, "Debbie shouldn't have said that to you. She dishonored you, Robert. You were the wronged spouse this time. You poor thing; you've really been mistreated."

That feeling is not from God. It's false comfort, and it's from the devil. Here's the rest of that lie as it often plays out between marriage partners. One of Satan's bunch says, "You'll never get over this, Robert. Just file this bruise away so you'll have some good ammunition the next time you get in an argument with her. You just saw your wife's true character. She's not right for you. Don't you wish you were with someone else right now?"

That's a lie from the pit of hell!

The problem is that too many Christians buy into that lie. They link arms with Satan at that point and say, "You know, you're right, Satan. I'm glad you're on my side. Thank you for being such an understanding and comforting friend." And they begin to nurse feelings of anger, resentment, malice, hate, jealousy, pride, and independence. They begin to feel that God has cheated them—that He set them up with the wrong marriage partner. "Maybe what needs to happen is a separation—doesn't it? Surely you can find comfort and respect in the arms of someone else." This is the point where that same whispering voice stops being a comforter and turns into a tormenter. A torturer. And that's where bruising becomes bondage.

It's no accident that Jesus came not just to heal the brokenhearted but also to liberate the bruised.

God's True Comfort

I mentioned before how I was picked on as a child by some bigger boys. I vowed I'd never be scared or pushed around again. You know what happened? One of Satan's bunch came to me and started falsely comforting me. He said, "You're right, Robert. You never again will get hurt. I'll be your comforter." And I let the devil be that to me. I held on to my anger and refused to forgive. Then a spirit of rage entered me, and my false comforter turned into my tormenter. Later, when I was in my teen years, I got into a fight with a guy, and I seriously hurt him.

That spirit of rage tormented me even after I got saved. Jesus had renewed my life (2 Corinthians 5:17), but the devil still had a legal right to harm me because of my unconfessed sin, which still so easily entangled me (Hebrews 12:1 NIV). That spirit tormented me in the first few years of my marriage too. I got angry at Debbie a lot, and it's a wonder she ever put up with me, but by God's grace she did.

Finally in prayer I revisited that place in my mind and heart when I first became wounded. With the help of a mentor, I was able to submit that bruised memory to the Holy Spirit. By the power of Christ working in me, I extended forgiveness to the bigger boys who'd picked on me. It didn't make what they'd done any less wrong. But it meant that I wasn't going to hold their sin against them anymore. The Holy Spirit healed that memory, and the Holy Spirit healed me.

Here's a twist to that story. As a boy, I'd made a vow never to show weakness again. Specifically, I convinced myself I was never going to cry. And I kept that vow for twenty-three years.

After I was healed, the mentor who'd led me through that time asked about any vows I'd made as a boy as part of my hurt. I told him about the no-crying vow. My mentor said, "As part of your healing, the Lord will soon lead you to a place and time where you will cry again."

I didn't know if I liked that, but I said okay. A while later I couldn't sleep one night. I had just gotten a new *Reader's Digest*, so I got up and began to read the funny parts, such as "Humor in Uniform," "Campus Comedy," and "Laughter Is the Best Medicine." I was about to set down the magazine and go back to bed when my eye caught a picture of a little girl standing beside a grave at a cemetery. The title of the article was, "When Daddy Doesn't Come Home."

My daughter was about the same age as the girl pictured in the article, and right away I thought, *I'm not reading that.* But the Holy Spirit said, *Oh yes you are.*

I started to bargain in prayer. I said, "Lord, if I read that article, it's going to hurt, and I don't want to hurt."

And the Lord said, *It's going to be okay, Robert. You're going to read it, and you're going to cry, and you're going to like it.*

You know how the articles in *Reader's Digest* are all purposely short? Well, that article took me two hours to read.

At times I could read only one word because I was crying so hard. I'd read a word, then set down the magazine and cry, then read another word and cry some more. I cried and cried. When I finally got through the article, the Lord said, *This has been part of your healing, Robert. The past is finally gone. You are truly free.*

Let's pray together right now. I'm going to ask the Holy Spirit to bring some memories to your mind right now that He wants to heal. Those memories will undoubtedly still be painful. Maybe you experienced a great loss. Or maybe something traumatic happened to you—verbal abuse, physical abuse, even sexual abuse. Maybe it's something that happened with a stranger, or maybe it involved a close friend or spouse or parent. Maybe you did something that you're still ashamed of, and the person you need to forgive is yourself.

Whatever that pain is, let's go to the Lord in prayer.

Lord Jesus Christ, You are the Healer and our true Comforter. You hold us in the palm of Your hand. Lord, right now we want to remember, in the power of Jesus' name, any emotional wounding that's happened to us, any great loss we've experienced, any wrong that's been done to us that we haven't forgiven. We want to purposely name in prayer the reason for the pain we feel. Lord, we bring that wounded and bruised experience to You and place it at Your feet. Father, we acknowledge to You this great hurt and pray specifically for holy forgetfulness. We submit these memories to You and ask that You would heal us.

Where there has been a lack of forgiveness, let there now be forgiveness in the power of Jesus' name. I choose now, by an act of my will, to forgive every person who has ever wronged me and to release bitterness and unforgiveness in Jesus' name. I choose to forgive myself for the wrong and shameful things I've done and to receive God's forgiveness through Jesus Christ.

Where we have held on to feelings of being hurt, please take those feelings now and remove them from our lives.

Where there are feelings of great loss, remind us that You hold all of life in Your sovereign hands.

In Jesus' name, we ask for deliverance from any demonic force that has influenced us. We ask that any footholds given the enemy would be removed from the enemy's hand. By the name of Jesus Christ, we command every spirit that's attached to these memories to flee—every spirit of insecurity, every spirit of fear, every spirit of anger, every spirit of bitterness or resentment or control or false independence, manipulation, rejection, or lack of forgiveness.

Fill us now to the full measure with all the goodness of God. We agree with the psalmist in prayer that You, O Lord, are our light and salvation—we have nobody and nothing to fear. You are the stronghold of our lives; we are not afraid anymore (Psalm 27:1). We pray that our hearts would not be troubled (John 14:1) and that we might receive the peace that You have for us (John 14:27). We ask that You, the God of all comfort, would fill us with joy and peace as we trust in You, so that we would overflow with hope by the power of the Holy Spirit (Romans 15:13).

We worship You, Lord, for You are sovereign. You are good. In Jesus Christ's name, amen.

Emotional healing can sometimes be a onetime process, and it can sometimes be a journey. Jesus walks with us on that journey, and He is our destination as well. I have found emotional healing to be extremely powerful in my own life. I pray that it will be in yours as well.

We're nearing the end of this book. There is just one more chapter to go, and then I'll give you some more resources in the back of the book that you can work through if you want. This final chapter is where we talk about becoming truly and finally free. It's the message many of you have been waiting for, one of the keys to starting down your road of freedom.

Questions for Contemplation or Group Discussion

1. Read Isaiah 61:1–4. What about these verses encourages you most, and why?
2. Why do you think the enemy tries so hard to bring things into our lives to cause us to be brokenhearted?
3. Why do people often have a hard time coming to God to find healing for their brokenness? What makes it hard for you to come to God?
4. Is there anyone who has hurt you whom you need to forgive?
5. The Bible says God is love. What are some of the ways God's love brings healing to our hearts?
6. Is there an area of your life where you've had a broken heart and God has healed you? Talk about it or write it in a journal.

Chapter Ten

A PRAYER FOR FREEDOM

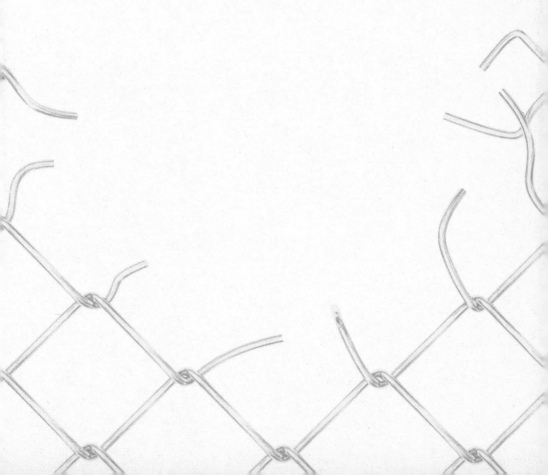

For you were called to freedom.

—GALATIANS 5:13 ESV

D ebbie and I once went to a seminar where we were instructed to read a small booklet about repentance, being forgiven, and forgiving others, and then to take any and all necessary steps in that process. Within the booklet were all sorts of questions designed to help a person identify sin in his or her life and then repent fully of that sin before God. If possible, that person was to make restitution.

We went back home, and Debbie took three hours to work through the booklet.

I took about fifteen minutes.

It wasn't because Debbie was more sinful than I was. Far from it. It was because I didn't take the process as seriously as I needed to.

That's what I want to point you to as we close this book. We've talked about the need for repentance throughout this book, but I want to underscore it here one last time so it sticks in your mind. Let me lay it out plainly: repentance, true repentance, is *crucial* for finding freedom from spiritual oppression. So I urge you to take this process seriously. Allow the Holy Spirit to convict you of sin, and then, by God's grace and power, fully repent of that sin. Don't gloss over anything in your relationship with God, particularly in the area of deliverance. If you want to become truly free, it may well take longer than fifteen minutes.

I realize that repentance isn't a popular word today, even in churches. It implies wrongdoing. Transgression. Sin. Yet I challenge us all to get past any baggage we may have surrounding this term and see repentance the way God sees it.

Repentance means that we agree with God and turn away from sin.

Repentance involves contrition and sorrow.

Repentance means we regret past actions because they were ultimately offenses against a holy and righteous God.

The good news about repentance is that the Holy Spirit helps us in our weaknesses—even in our repenting. If we find ourselves struggling with repentance, we are invited to pray for God's help in changing our hearts, in seeing our sins for what they truly are—reprehensible to God—and in grabbing hold of the amazing grace and forgiveness He always offers us.

I hope you've come to see throughout this book that becoming free may not happen exactly in the same way for everyone. For me, after I realized fifteen minutes wasn't going to cut it, I found that the process proved to be much more of a journey.

I needed to go through some deep seasons of surrendering to God so He could clean up some things in my past. I had people I needed to forgive, and I had people from whom I needed to ask their forgiveness. All that took time.

In the past I had resisted many of these actions and attitudes of the heart, but in that time of sincere repentance, I was struck with the idea that repentance is only effective if it is thorough. I also found I needed someone to help me through my issues, to fervently pray with me and for me and over me in these areas. By God's grace, I am now truly free.

What will your journey of deliverance be like? It will undoubtedly look different from mine. So let's recap the main themes of this book, and put together some ideas for where you might go from here.

Your Journey of Deliverance

We've talked through three main themes in this book.

First, demonic oppression is real, and it's more common than we think. This problem happens to everyday people, people just like you and me, and it affects believers as well as nonbelievers. The good part is that Jesus both calls us to be free and offers the key to true freedom.

Second, deliverance is needed along with discipleship for any believer to go forward spiritually and become truly free. Too many people, even believers, never get delivered from bondage because they cannot understand how it works or don't realize it's even possible for a Christian to be spiritually oppressed. We've talked about how leaving open a door or window in our house might allow a thief to come in. He wouldn't own the house, but he would still be inside, bringing fear or terror or evil with him and influencing what happens within the walls. Sin can open up the doors of our lives to demonic activity, and once the doors are open, those spirits have the legal right to come and negatively influence us. Our sins must be repented of and the demonic spirits cast out, not in a spooky way but in an authoritative way, in the name of the Lord Jesus Christ.

The third main theme of this book has been that God offers big hope to anyone seeking deliverance. God is greater and more powerful than all the spiritual hosts that exist, and when God is sought, God is found (Jeremiah 29:13).

In this final chapter we want to draw together all three of these main themes and offer four specific steps you can take to find true freedom. Additionally, as I've mentioned, God is not bound by time or space or the pages of a book, so I'll pray for you extensively at the end of the chapter. I'll also leave you with some extended resources in the appendix. I encourage you not to overlook this section of the book.

Do you want to be truly free? This is the chapter I've been waiting for, one that points us down the road of freedom. I bet you've been waiting for it too.

Let's look at four steps to becoming set free. By outlining these simple steps, I'm not trying to oversimplify the process or trivializing it in any way. I'm just trying to make the process straightforward. Think of these four steps as signposts along your pathway. If you want to be free, then walk the following direction:

Step #1: Recognize You Need Help

Most of us are familiar with the story of the prodigal son as found in Luke 15. A man had two sons, and the younger son decided to go his own way. He asked his father to divide the inheritance, took the portion that one day would be his, and journeyed to a far-off country, where he wasted his inheritance in immoral living.

After the younger son had squandered all he had, a famine arose in the land where he was staying. The son was penniless by this point. None of his former friends would help, so he hired himself out to a pig farmer who paid extremely poorly. The son lived in the pigpen and was often so hungry that the pig slop looked tasty to him.

Finally, Luke wrote, the son "came to his senses" (v. 17 NIV) and he made a plan to go home to his father.

In other words, he recognized he needed help. And at that point his restoration began.

Do you recognize you need help? It's a simple question with profound and far-reaching ramifications.

Many people—believers and unbelievers—live in pigpens. That's picture language for a messy, chaotic life. Sometimes the mess is evident on the outside. Sometimes outsiders would never know. Either way, these people are not where they should be. Their lives are mucky wallows of hunger, cold, anguish, fear, anger, regret, loneliness, exhaustion, sorrow, and stress.

But here's the good news. None of us have to live in our pigpens. In more than thirty years of ministry, the only people I've ever seen who can't get free of their pigsties are the people who won't admit they have a problem.

That's step one. Recognize you need help.

Step #2: Repent to God and Others

Do you want to be set free? There's a condition. Repentance is a must, just as we talked about at the start of this chapter.

After the prodigal son realized his need, he chose to repent. Luke 15:18 records his plan: "I will arise and go to my father, and will say to him, 'Father, I have sinned against heaven and before you.'"

And do you know what happened when the prodigal son came home and said those words to his father? The father welcomed his repentant son with wide-open arms and restored him to the family.

Misunderstandings abound when it comes to repentance. The biggest is that repentance is the same as confession. The two are related, but they are not the same.

A person can confess a sin glibly. He can say, "Oh sure, I did it." But that does not mean there is any contriteness in his heart. True repentance involves sorrow. It acknowledges a sinful act or attitude for what it is: an abomination against an absolutely holy and righteous God.

The Greek word for repentance, *metanoia*, comes from two Greek words. The first is *meta*, which is properly translated "after" or "with" but "implying change afterward."[1] The second is *noia*, which refers to the mind. Literally, repentance means "a change of mind,"[2] "a complete change of thought and attitude."[3]

When we repent, we change our minds about several things:

- We change our minds about sin. We are heading one way and then change direction.
- We change our minds about ourselves. We acknowledge that when we engage in sin, we are not being the people God created us to be.
- We also change our minds about God. God is not just some divine Rule Maker up in the sky, waiting for us to mess up so He can bop us on our heads. God is a loving God who always welcomes us home with open arms.

I've heard some Christians say that once we get saved, we never need to repent again. That's incorrect. Repentance is both a onetime act that we do at our salvation and an ongoing act that we need to do on a regular basis. (If believers don't need to repent, then Jesus used the wrong word in Revelation 2–3 when He called five of the seven churches in Asia Minor to repentance.)

For believers, I actually recommend repenting daily. It's a good thing to keep short accounts with God.

What happens when we come to God in repentance? The father's response to the prodigal son gives us a wonderful picture of a heavenly Father who watches eagerly for us to return to Him. First John 1:9 describes it this way: "If we confess our sins, He is faithful and just to forgive us our sins and to cleanse us from all unrighteousness."

The power to repent always comes from the Holy Spirit. For unbelievers, the Holy Spirit quickens their hearts to be able to turn toward God. For believers, the Holy Spirit helps us admit where we've strayed and turn back around. Yes, it requires our willingness to go along with God. But the real work is always done by Him.

Numbers 21:8 models this truth about repentance. After the Israelites sinned in the wilderness and were punished by biting serpents, the Lord said to Moses, "Make a snake and put it up on a pole; anyone who is bitten can look at it and live" (NIV). The people didn't need to shine themselves up to repent. They didn't need to "get right" first or get their acts together. All they needed to do was look. God did the real work in creating new hearts within them.

Jesus repeated this process in relation to Himself in John 3:14, saying, "Just as Moses lifted up the snake in the wilderness, so the Son of Man must be lifted up" (NIV). That means all we need to do is look at the Son—really see who He is—to be transformed. In John 6:40, Jesus added to this idea: "For this is the will of my Father, that everyone who *looks on the Son* and believes in him should have eternal life" (ESV).

As simple as repentance is, however, we still must choose to do it. It requires our agreeing with God and changing our minds about sin. It also means *admitting* that sin to God and to ourselves. Confession may not be the same thing as repentance, but it's hard to have genuine repentance without some form of confession.

Repentance is something that happens first between an individual and God. Wherever possible, however, it's a good thing to involve other people in the process. In the story of the prodigal son, the son confesses his sin and expresses his repentance to his earthly father as well as to God and himself.

Sometimes the other people we involve in our repentance will be the ones who have been harmed by our sins. They will need to hear our confessions and apologies as part of their healing processes. And sometimes the "other people" will be trusted spiritual friends. This is simply because freedom from guilt is often processed better within community.

Matthew 5:23–24 drives home this point: "Therefore if you bring your gift to the altar, and there remember that your brother has something against you, leave your gift there before the altar, and go your way. First be reconciled to your brother, and then come and offer your gift." In other words, God says, "If you want to get right with Me, get right with your brother first. Then come get right with Me."

James 5:16 bolsters this, telling us to "confess your trespasses to one another, and pray for one another, that you may be healed." The definition of the Greek word translated *healed* means "to free from errors and sins."[4] Another way to put this verse is like this: "Confess your sins to one another that you may be free."

When you confess your sin to others, I do recommend you do it only with those people who are affected by it. That means either the person who's been affected or those with whom you are in close fellowship. For a while in church circles it was popular to have mass confessions, where an open microphone would be offered, and anyone who wanted could get up in front of a crowd and lay bare his or her heart. That made for some awkward meetings, let me tell you.

In my experience it's far better to keep the group small. Confess to your pastor, your small-group leader or the people in your small group, your mentor, your Bible study group, or your accountability partner. If you're married, confess to your spouse. The main point is to confess. When it comes to sin, bring that sin out into the light. Satan loves darkness and does his most effective work there.

Step #3: Renounce the Lies of Satan

All bondage begins with a lie. To find freedom, therefore, we need to expose the lies, to see them for what they are and clean them out of our heads. We must turn around former misconceptions so we can see truth and fill our minds with the good things of God. And to do this we must soak our minds with scriptures. We must set ourselves up to "be transformed by the *renewing of [our minds]*" (Romans 12:2) so we continue to see through the lies Satan tries out on us.

Luke 15:25–29 describes something that happened after the prodigal son came home and the father welcomed him back. It concerns the response of his older brother.

> Now his older son was in the field, and as he came and drew near to the house, he heard music and dancing. And he called one of the servants and asked what these things meant. And he said to him, "Your brother has come, and your father has killed the fattened calf, because he has received him back safe and sound." But he was angry and refused to go in. His father came out and entreated him, but he answered his father, "Look, these many years I have served you, and I never disobeyed your command, yet you never gave me a young goat, that I might celebrate with my friends." (ESV)

Notice the absolutes the older brother tried out on the father. "I *never* disobeyed your command." "You *never* gave me a young goat."

That's two big lies, right off the bat.

It's certainly untrue that the older brother had never disobeyed his father. If you have children, you know there's no such thing as a child who *never* disobeys.

But the older son also claimed that his father *never* gave him a goat—the implication is that the father had never given him anything. But back in Luke 15:12, the father divided the inheritance at the younger son's request, and the text says, "So he divided to them his livelihood."

Did you catch that? The father divided it to *them*. The older brother had already received his share. Because he was older, he'd actually gotten twice as much as the younger brother. The older brother was rich!

The father's gracious reply in Luke 15:31 frames it well: "Son, you are always with me, and all that I have is yours." He was saying, "Son, you were here with me the whole time. You had everything." But the son couldn't see it because his head was clouded with lies.

Here's the problem: The older son never left home as the younger son had done, but the older brother was still in bondage. He wasn't in bondage to the upstroke of wild living or to the downstroke of the pigpen. But he was in bondage to bitterness, resentment, hate, jealousy, envy, and a lack of forgiveness.

How many of us are in exactly the same position? We might never have strayed far from the course of righteous living, but we're still in bondage to lies about who we are and where we belong.

My wife, Debbie, was talking with her sister, Mari, one day about their growing-up years with their mom and dad. (My mother-in-law now lives near us in Dallas. Debbie's father has gone on to be with the Lord.) The two sisters agreed that they'd had a great childhood. But in the course of that conversation, they also realized that, at some point, each of them had believed the other was the parents' favorite. That surfaced some old feelings of resentment. When they sorted it out, they had a good laugh about it, and some good-natured repentance took place too.

A lot of people can point to similar family misunderstandings and dynamics. Some are minor and even funny—in retrospect, at least.

But some are serious sources of lifelong pain and represent serious bondage. Have you ever heard something like this? "Well, I'm the oldest child, so I always need to be in control." To that I would ask, why don't you just say it plainly? Just say, "I have a demon of control." Or they say, "I'm the youngest child, so I always need to have my way." To which, I ask, "Well, why don't you just say, 'I have a demon of selfishness'"? Or they say, "Well, I'm the middle child, so I'm the neglected one." Or "I'm an only child, so that means I'm self-centered." We need to repent of this kind of thinking and renounce the lies of Satan!

Here's the truth that God's Word lays out plainly for us: As believers we've been adopted into a new family. It doesn't matter what family we grew up in. We're in a new family.

The Bible tells us who we are. We're children of God. We're born again by the Word of God, kept by the power of God, sealed by the Holy Spirit until the day of redemption. God has put all things under our feet. He has given us authority over all the power of the enemy. We're more than conquerors through Christ. We always triumph in Him. Greater is He that is in us than he that is in the world.

That's the truth that drives out all the lies. The truth that makes us truly free.

Step #4: Receive the Gifts of the Father

The prodigal son received three specific gifts from his father in Luke 15:22:

- a robe—and not just any old robe, but the best in the house
- a ring
- sandals for his feet

These presents symbolized the father's love for his son and the openhearted forgiveness of the father. But for us, those who are moving toward true freedom in Christ, the gifts in this story also remind us what our heavenly Father bestows when we turn from our sins, ask for deliverance, and claim our rightful place as His beloved children.

What do the presents represent in this context?

The robe is a covering garment. It clothes a person in dignity and in newness. It brings to mind the robe of righteousness described in Isaiah 61:10:

> *I will greatly rejoice in the* LORD,
> *My soul shall be joyful in my God;*
> *For He has clothed me with the garments of salvation,*
> *He has covered me with the robe of righteousness,*
> *As a bridegroom decks himself with ornaments,*
> *And as a bride adorns herself with her jewels.*

If we're going to be free, then we need to receive the righteousness of God. That righteousness doesn't come by anything we do. It's all because of what Jesus did on the cross.

A ring was a sign of authority in biblical times. It signified that the person wearing the ring had been granted position, honor, power, and responsibility.

When Pharaoh established Joseph as second-in-command over all Egypt, he put a ring on his hand (Genesis 41:42). When King Ahasuerus was tricked by Haman into letting him harass the Jews in Susa, the king "took his signet ring from his hand and gave it to Haman" (Esther 3:10). When King Darius threw Daniel into the lions' den, "a stone was brought and laid on the mouth of the den, and the king sealed it with his own signet ring and with the signets of his lords, that the purpose concerning Daniel might not be changed" (Daniel 6:17).

Jesus grants us His authority in Luke 10:19—not to do evil but to do good: "Behold, I give you the authority to trample on serpents and scorpions." Within the context of that passage, those are demonic spirits we have authority over, not desert animals. Through the name of Jesus

Christ, we have been given all power over evil spirits. We have God's authority over the enemy.

But what about shoes? Shoes are what protect our feet. They help us go places. They help us do things. And in that sense they represent power.

The gift of power that God gives us is not *something*. It's *Someone*, the Holy Spirit. Acts 1:8 says, "You shall receive power when the Holy Spirit has come upon you." God has given us the gift of His Holy Spirit. We need to continually be filled with the Spirit's presence, and that power is available if we only ask.

All of us recognize areas of struggle, weakness, and probably bondage in our lives. The good news is: Greater is He! "Greater is he that is in you, than he that is in the world" (1 John 4:4 KJV). If we will recognize our need for help, repent to God and others, renounce the lies of the enemy, and receive the freedom Jesus died to give us and the power the Holy Spirit brings us, we can be free, truly free!

Freedom Prayers

In closing let's spend some time praying right now. If there's any bondage in your life, don't you want to get free? Of course! So let's go to the Father in prayer.

At first I suggest you spend a few moments in repentance. Ask the Lord to bring to mind any sins that have caused bondage in your life. It might be small things. It might be big things. Confess them out loud or on paper.

This process may take a few moments or much longer. You may need to call someone or write someone a letter. You may need to work through some issues with a trusted spiritual friend or counselor. But do whatever it takes. Open your eyes to the sin in your life, the ways you have opened yourself up to Satan's influence. Then take a moment to say out loud, "Lord Jesus, I repent."

Now let's pray. You may want to read these words out loud:

Father, I ask You to forgive me for all of my sin, and I ask You to release me from every bondage, in Jesus' name.

Next, I want to pray for you and over you.

Lord, right now, by the authority You have given me, I take authority over Satan, and I address every demonic spirit that has held my brothers and sisters in bondage. I do this in Jesus' name, and in His name I command you to go. In Jesus' name! It is not the authority of my voice or the words on this paper. It is by the authority of the Lord Jesus Christ.

My brothers and sisters are covered by the blood of the Lamb. They have overcome by the word of their testimony and belief in Jesus Christ. They are born again, not of corruptible seed but of incorruptible seed that lives and abides forever. The Word of God is living and active and sharper than any two-edged sword. It's sweeter than honey and purer than gold. And in the name of Jesus, by the Word of God and by the blood of the Lamb, my brothers and sisters are set free today.

I take authority over every spirit of bitterness or unforgiveness or resentment or hate or malice or envy or jealousy, and I command you in Jesus' name to go right now.

I rebuke every spirit of insecurity or inferiority, fear, rejection, self-hate, self-pity, or self-destruction in Jesus' name. Suicide, I command you in the name of Jesus to go right now.

Every spirit of anger or rage or murder or violence or lawlessness, I command you in Jesus' name to go.

Every spirit of sexual immorality, adultery, fornication, lust, pornography—all forms of sexual impurity—in the name of Jesus, I command you to go right now.

Every spirit of pride or lying, every Jezebel spirit, every spirit of deception, manipulation, or control, I command you in Jesus' name to go.

Every spirit of criticism, judgmentalism, arrogance, prejudice, or racism, I command you in the name of Jesus to go.

Every spirit of greed, materialism, selfishness, covetousness, or selfish ambition, in Jesus' name I command you to go.

Depression, anxiety, worry, in Jesus' name, I command you to go.

Addiction, alcoholism, drunkenness, drugs, gluttony, in Jesus' name I command you to go.

Every spirit of legalism or religious pride or heresy or false doctrine, in Jesus' name I command you to go.

Every spirit of stealing or slothfulness or laziness, unbelief, rebellion to authority, in Jesus' name I command you to go.

Every spirit of guilt, shame, embarrassment, humiliation, in Jesus' name I command you to go.

Every spirit of sickness or disease, infirmities, chronic health issues, in Jesus' name I command you to go.

Every spirit of witchcraft or the occult or blasphemy, in Jesus' name I command you to go.

In the name of Jesus I break every word, curse, and spell spoken over my brothers or sisters. Every generational curse, in Jesus' name I command you to go right now.

Every demonic spirit that has held my brothers and sisters in bondage, in Jesus' name I command you to go right now.

Take another minute to pray for the filling of the Holy Spirit. Read this out loud, too, if you'd like:

Lord, please fill me to the full measure with Your Holy Spirit. Every place that evil spirits have left, please fill with the Holy Spirit, in Jesus' name. I want You—and only You—in my life.

I'll pray that for you too.

Lord, I ask You to fill this person with the Holy Spirit right now from the top of the head to the bottom of the feet. We receive You in Jesus' name. Amen! Amen!

What the Lord has accomplished in your heart today is truly strong and mighty. May this healing that He has freely given be sealed in your heart. May the gifts He has given you today stay with you always.

Let's close this book by continuing in the attitude and posture of prayer.

Lord Jesus Christ, we rebuke the attack of the enemy that would come to take what is rightfully ours. Neither man nor woman nor circumstance nor time can take what the Creator has given to us today.

I declare the blood of Christ over every person who reads this book. We thank You, God, with humble hearts for Your grace, Your mercy, Your loving-kindness.

May everyone who reads this book be protected, in Jesus' name. May God guide each person through the wilderness and protect him or her through the storm.

We declare in prayer that the One who watches over us neither sleeps nor slumbers. He vigilantly protects us and mercilessly avenges us. May we always be in the protection of His wings.

> Christ be with you, Christ within you,
> Christ before you, Christ behind you,
> Christ on your right, Christ on your left,
> Christ above you, Christ beneath you,
> Christ around you, right now and forevermore.

Almighty God, heavenly Father, breathe Your Holy Spirit into our hearts and into our spirits.

May we, fearing only You, have no other fear. Knowing Your compassion, may we be ever mindful of Your love. And serving You faithfully unto death, may we live eternally with You.

We thank You today and pray all these things in the name of the Father and the Son and the Holy Spirit. Amen.

Questions for Contemplation or Group Discussion

1. Why do people have trouble admitting they're in bondage?

2. Which of the two sons do you most identify with in the parable?

3. Read James 5:16. Confessing our sins to another person is humbling and can be painful. Have you ever confessed your sins to someone else, then experienced the healing that comes from doing this? Explain if you're comfortable.

4. What are some of the lies that Satan tells us about who we are? In practical terms, how do we renounce these lies?

5. Beautiful imagery is given in Scripture about a robe of righteousness, a ring of authority, and the gift of power (the Holy Spirit). How do these three gifts help us to be set free?

Appendix

RESOURCES FOR
YOU TO USE

Making Sure You're Born Again

M aking sure you're a Christian is central to your journey to freedom. To be truly set free, you must first have a clear picture of your new identity in Christ. Confidence of salvation is stated clearly in Scripture:

> And this is the testimony: that God has given us eternal life, and this life is in His Son. He who has the Son has life; he who does not have the Son of God does not have life. These things I have written to you who believe in the name of the Son of God, that you may know that you have eternal life, and that you may continue to believe in the name of the Son of God. (1 John 5:11–13)

If you have not followed Christ yet or if you don't know for sure whether you have or have not, then prayerfully read the following verses that explain what it means to become a Christian and how to do so:

- Romans 3:23
- Romans 10:10
- John 3:16–17
- Ephesians 2:8–9
- Titus 3:5
- 2 Corinthians 13:5
- Matthew 7:13–23

- Hebrews 6:1–8
- John 15:7

You receive Jesus Christ by believing in your heart that He is the Son of God and the Redeemer of mankind, and by orally confessing your love and commitment to Him. These two responses constitute the act of receiving faith (Romans 10:10). Consider saying the following prayer:

Dear God, I confess to You that I have sinned and ask You to forgive me now for all of my sins. I believe that Jesus Christ is Your Son, that He died on the cross, and that He rose from the grave on the third day. I receive You today as my Lord and Savior. Thank You, Jesus, for saving me today! In Jesus' name, amen.

When you pray a prayer like that and mean what you say, God then places His Spirit inside you and makes you a new creation (2 Corinthians 5:17). The foundational issue of your identity is resolved by the single step of being born again. You can then begin the process of growth and of renewing your mind.

Frequently Asked Questions About Deliverance

1. How can you tell whether a problem is demonically related, or caused by something else?

The main way that we can tell if a problem is demonically related is the inability to overcome it on our own. We tell God over and over that we will never do it again, but we continue to feel trapped in that area. No self-will or discipline on our own seems to help. Jesus stated that the woman in Luke 13:10–17 had a spirit of infirmity and that Satan had her bound and she could not raise herself up. The three main doors that either open a person to demonic activity or are signs of demonic activity are continued willful sinning, continued illness without an apparent reason, and participation in the occult.

2. What are the key steps to being delivered?

Once a person realizes his or her need for deliverance, the key steps are: repentance, prayers for deliverance, filling of the Holy Spirit, and biblical meditation to renew the mind.

3. Can a person pray for deliverance on his or her own, or is it necessary to go to a pastor or spiritual mentor and have that person pray?

A person can pray for deliverance on his or her own, yet it is often beneficial and recommended for that person to be prayed for within a community of believers with spiritual leadership present.

4. If a person prays for deliverance but the problem continues, what then?

Ask the Holy Spirit to show you what is standing in the way of your freedom. Is there unconfessed sin? Is there something present in your life that gives demons a legal right to influence you? Do you need to forgive someone? Deliverance is part of the ongoing process of following Christ. Deliverance can be both a onetime event and part of the ongoing process of healing. If the problem continues, then it is wise to seek the counsel and direction of spiritual leaders.

5. If a person is delivered but then lapses back into sin, will demons return?

Hebrews 12:1–2 is clear that some sins can easily ensnare or entangle a person. Demonic activity may or may not occur as a result. Matthew 12:43–45 offers a picture of spiritual warfare in which a person is delivered from demonic activity but then persists in unbelief. A larger contingent of demons then goes on the attack. Jesus Christ, however, is always greater than Satan and his bunch (1 John 4:4).

6. Can a person anonymously pray for other people whom he or she suspects are being demonically oppressed? If so, will deliverance occur?

Certainly a person can pray with authority for anything in Jesus' name that's in accordance with God's will. For instance, a person might pray for the cleansing of a city or for the deliverance of a friend or relative who hasn't been in contact for a while. At the same time, deliverance is not a guarantee in those situations because a person must, by his or her will, want to become free. Prayer is always recommended, though, because we know that God always hears our prayers (1 John 5:15).

7. Can demons inhabit a certain region or a certain space, such as a room in a house? What can be done about this?

Scripture is clear that some demons are territorial demons (Daniel 10:12–13; Mark 5:8–13). It is right and good to pray for spiritual cleansing of rooms in a house—when you move into a new residence, for instance, or even when you get a hotel room for the night. In the name of Jesus Christ, command any demonic presences to go where Jesus would send them. Ask the Holy Spirit to fill the room or region with His sweet, peaceful, and powerful presence. In your own home make sure there are no articles of false worship or any articles of overt sin. If so, remove the articles, throw them away, or destroy them. You may want to use the following suggested prayer:

Heavenly Father, I acknowledge that You are Lord of heaven and earth. In Your sovereign power and love, You have given me all things richly to enjoy. Thank You for this place to live. In Jesus' name, I cleanse this home for my family as a place of spiritual safety and protection from all attacks of the enemy.

As a child of God seated with Christ in the heavenly realm, I command every evil spirit claiming ground in the structures and furnishings of this place to leave and never return. I renounce all curses and spells utilized against this place.

I ask You, heavenly Father, to post guardian angels around this home, to guard it from attempts of the enemy to enter and disturb Your purposes for me. I thank You, Lord, for doing this and pray in the name of the Lord Jesus Christ, amen.

8. If a person is sick and demonic activity is suspected as the cause, what course of action should be taken?

The same steps for any ministry of deliverance are the same—confession, prayers for deliverance, filling of the Holy Spirit, and biblical meditation. Additionally, James 5:14–16 calls for church elders to anoint the sick person with oil to pray over him. Take this verse literally. In other words, call your church's elders or spiritual leaders and have them dab some olive oil or cooking oil on the forehead of the sick person, then pray for healing. You may want to use the following suggested prayer:

Heavenly Father, Your Word says in Exodus 15:26 that You are the Lord who heals people. Today, Lord, we proclaim that the same resurrection power that raised Christ from the dead is flooding [say person's name]'s body with healing. We rebuke Satan and every demonic spirit that is coming against [say person's name], in Jesus' name.

In the name of Jesus, we pray that none of the following symptoms, [list symptoms], would be present anymore, and that [say person's name] would be healed and made well. Lord, we ask that every cell, tissue, and organ in his [her] body would function in the perfection in which You created it.

We thank You, Lord, that right now [say person's name]'s body is lining up with Your Word and receiving health and healing right now. Thank You for being our ever-present help in times of need. In Jesus' name we pray, amen.

9. Can children be demonically oppressed? If so, what should parents or caregivers do about it?

Scripture shows several examples of children being demonically oppressed, whether from their own sin or from being in an environment of overt sin. Follow the same steps for deliverance for children as you would for an adult.

Great care needs to be taken with children to ensure they are not frightened by the experience of being prayed for in a deliverance context. Keep the number of people who pray for the child to a minimum. Keep your voice low, calm, and peaceful. Reassure the children through scriptures that Christ is greater than any demon (1 John 4:4) and that they are not bad because the devil is attacking them. You can point out that the devil attacked Jesus also, and we know that He was not a bad person.

Note that there are always secular legal issues surrounding the care of children, so great care must be taken to follow local, regional, and federal laws, particularly if you are a caregiver and not a parent. For instance, a Sunday school teacher or youth worker should not pray for direct deliverance of a child or teen unless the child's parents or legal guardians are present or have been notified and are in agreement.

If you are a parent yourself, then pray regularly for your children's protection in spiritual realms. If your children are believers, pray that your children would be filled to the full measure with God's Holy Spirit.

10. How can a person break any unhealthy connections he or she may have developed within the course of a previous romantic relationship?

We call these unhealthy connections "soul ties," and they can occur if people have participated in sexual relationships outside the boundaries of marriage.

The sexual relationship in a marriage covenant is designed to create a significant bond and knit together two people into one. Sexual relationships are designed by God for the union of the mind, body, emotions, and spirit. This connection isn't limited to intercourse. Any interaction that engages the sexual drives can create such a connection. Freedom from sexual sin requires the added step of submitting this tie to the Lord to sever any unholy and unhealthy connections.

You may want to use the following prayer:

Dear Lord, I confess that I have engaged in sexual activity outside of marriage, and I acknowledge this as sin. I developed a sexual connection with (say person's name), and I ask You to break any soul tie that was created between this person and me. I ask You to restore to me anything that was lost or taken during these sexual connections, and I pray that You would remove any detriment that has stayed with me since the time of these connections. Your Word says You are a God of restoration, so I now ask that You restore my purity and make me clean in Your eyes and in my eyes as well. I thank You for the work You are doing in me and pray that You would seal it by the power of the Holy Spirit. In Jesus' name, amen.

11. Can people be demonically oppressed because of something done by their parents, grandparents, or ancestors?

Yes. Generational iniquity is simply a predisposition, inherited from ancestors, to certain sins. Even after personal sins have been dealt with, troubling patterns and circumstances in your life can still continue. Generational sins are passed down through the examples of behavior you saw as a young person, through "spiritual genes," and through the law of sowing and reaping (Galatians 6:7–8). You may need to spiritually deal with any patterns of sin that have been passed down from your forebears.

We are accountable for the sins and iniquities that we commit. We are not guilty of the sins of our forefathers or responsible for what others have done on their own in the past. Yet that doesn't rule out the fact that we are heavily influenced by the environment in which we were raised. We are given the choice to walk in righteousness or yield to the bent of our ancestors' tendencies toward particular sins.

What areas of sin, rebellion, or occult activity have past generations of your family embraced? What kinds of sickness and disease have been evidenced in your family? If you recognize an issue of generational iniquity but don't know its source, ask the Holy Spirit to guide you into all truth (John 14:16–17).

Breaking generational iniquity begins with a desire to see change in yourself and in members of your family. The process isn't weird, mystical, or superstitious. What's involved in obtaining such deliverance is confessing the sins and iniquities of your ancestors (Exodus 20:5–6) and asking Jesus to cleanse your bloodlines to break any resulting curses and demonic activity.

You may want to pray using the following words:

Thank You, Lord Jesus, for my father, my mother, and the generations who have gone before me. Thank You for the good I've reaped because of their labors. I confess that I come from a family that is less than perfect. I understand that the sins and iniquities of my ancestors influence my own spiritual heritage. I acknowledge this heritage to You today in order to receive Your promise of cleansing and restoration (Leviticus 16).

The sins and iniquities of my ancestors include [name the sins and iniquities]. Heavenly Father, although these sins were once a part of my inheritance, I renounce them all in Jesus' name, and I renounce any demonic involvement that has influenced my life as a result. I cover my past and my heritage with the blood of Jesus.

I confess that these sins have now been cut off and cleansed from me by the blood of Your Son, Jesus. I also state in prayer that I have been made a new creation in Christ and have been given a new heritage. I claim my new heritage in Christ.

Thank You for giving me, my children, and my future descendants a new heritage and a new future. In Jesus' name, amen.

Ministry of Deliverance and Corresponding Infilling of the Holy Spirit

REBUKE AND CAST OUT	SCRIPTURE REFERENCE	RECEIVE AN INFILLING OF THE HOLY SPIRIT FOR	SCRIPTURE REFERENCE
Spirit of infirmity	Luke 13:11	Life, healing	Romans 8:2; 1 Corinthians 12:9
Spirit of fear	2 Timothy 1:6–7	Faith, love, power, sound mind	2 Timothy 1:7
Spirit of divination	Acts 16:16–18	Gifts of the Spirit	1 Corinthians 12:9–12
Spirit of harlotry	Hosea 4:12	Purity	Philippians 4:8
Spirit of bondage	Romans 8:15	Liberty	Romans 8:15
Haughty spirit	Proverbs 16:18–19	Humility	Proverbs 16:19; Colossians 3:12
Perverse spirit	Isaiah 19:14	Holiness	Zechariah 12:10; Romans 1:4
Spirit of the Antichrist	1 John 4:3	Truth	1 John 4:6
Deaf and mute spirit	Mark 9:25–27	Ability to hear and understand God's voice	Romans 8:11; 1 Corinthians 12:9
Lying spirit	2 Chronicles 18:22	Praise	Isaiah 61:3; Romans 15:13
Spirit of heaviness	Isaiah 61:3	Honesty	John 14:17; 15:26; 16:13
Spirit of jealousy	Numbers 5:14	Love of God	1 Corinthians 13; Ephesians 5:2
Spirit of stupor	Romans 11:8	Clarity of mind and heart	2 Timothy 1:7; Matthew 5:8
Spirit of error	1 John 4:6	Truthfulness, correctness	Psalm 51:10; John 16:13

Further Reading for Maintaining Your Victory

Neil T. Anderson

- *Living Free in Christ: The Truth About Who You Are and How Christ Can Meet Your Deepest Needs.* Ventura, CA: Gospel Light, 1993.
- *The Bondage Breaker: Overcoming Negative Thoughts, Irrational Feelings, Habitual Sins.* Eugene, OR: Harvest House, 2006. Originally published 1997.
- *Victory over the Darkness: Realizing the Power of Your Identity in Christ.* Ventura, CA: Regal, 2010. First published 1990.
- *Walking in the Light: Discerning God's Guidance in an Age of Spiritual Counterfeits.* Nashville: Thomas Nelson, 1993.

Neil T. Anderson with Joanne Anderson

- *Daily in Christ: A Devotional.* Eugene, OR: Harvest House, 2000. Originally published 1993.

Neil T. Anderson and Rich Miller

- *Freedom from Fear: Overcoming Worry and Anxiety.* Eugene, OR: Harvest House, 1999.

Jimmy Evans

- *A Mind Set Free: Overcoming Mental Strongholds Through Biblical Meditation.* Amarillo, TX: Marriage Today, 2000, 2004, 2007.

- *When Life Hurts: Finding Hope and Healing from the Pain You Carry*. Ada, MI: Baker Books, 2013.

Jimmy Evans and Ann Billington
- *Freedom From Your Past: A Christian Guide to Personal Healing and Restoration*. Amarillo, TX: Marriage Today, 1994, 2006, 2009.

Jack Hayford
- *Fatal Attractions: Why Sex Sins Are Worse Than Others*. Ventura, CA: Regal, 2004.
- *The Heart of Praise: Worship After God's Own Heart*. Ventura, CA: Regal, 1992, 2005.
- *Worship His Majesty: How Praising the King of Kings Will Change Your Life*, rev. ed. Ventura, CA: Regal, 2000.

Charles Kraft
- *Defeating Dark Angels: Breaking Demonic Oppression in the Believer's Life*. Ventura, CA: Regal, 1992, 2011.

Joyce Meyer
- *Battlefield of the Mind: Winning the Battle in Your Mind*, upd. commemorative ed. New York: FaithWords, 2011. Originally published 1995 by Harrison House.
- *Beauty for Ashes: Receiving Emotional Healing*. New York: FaithWords, 2002. Originally published 1994 by Harrison House.
- *The Battle Belongs to the Lord: Overcoming Life's Struggles Through Worship*. New York: FaithWords, 2002. Originally published 1982 by Harrison House.

Beth Moore
- *Breaking Free: Discover the Victory of Total Surrender*. Nashville: B&H Publishing Group, 2000, 2007.

- *Praying God's Word: Breaking Free from Spiritual Strongholds.* Nashville: B&H Publishing Group, 2000, 2009.

Robert Morris

- *The Power of Your Words: God Will Bless Your Life Through the Words You Speak.* Bloomington, MN: Bethany House, 2009, 2014.

Stormie Omartian

- *Finding Peace for Your Heart: A Woman's Guide to Emotional Health.* Nashville: Thomas Nelson, 1991.
- *Lord, I Want to Be Whole: The Power of Prayer and Scripture in Emotional Healing.* Nashville: Thomas Nelson, 2000.

ACKNOWLEDGMENT

I want to acknowledge Marcus Brotherton, without whose help I would not have been able to communicate what was in my heart as clearly and as effectively. You are a dear friend, and it was a joy to work with you!

NOTES

Chapter 1: Greater Is He

1. C. S. Lewis, *The Screwtape Letters*, repr. ed. (New York: HarperOne, 2009), ix.
2. Jack Hayford, lecture, School of Pastoral Nurture, The Kings University, fall 2006.
3. *Zomai* is a derivative of the word *ktaomai*, which is used in Luke 21:19, and is spelled *zomai* only when it is combined with the word *daimoni*. James Strong, *Enhanced Strong's Lexicon* (Bellingham, WA: Logos Bible Software, 2001): "to be under the power of a demon."
4. *Vine's Expository Dictionary of Biblical Words* (Nashville: Thomas Nelson, 1985): *ktaomai* (kta/omai, NT:2932), "to procure for oneself, acquire, obtain," hence, "to possess."
5. Johannes P. Louw and Eugene Nida, *Greek-English Lexicon of the New Testament Based on Semantic Domains*, Logos Bible Software (New York: United Bible Societies, 1996): 12.41, "to be possessed by a demon—'to be demon possessed.'"
6. Strong, *Enhanced Strong's Lexicon*: 5117.
7. Hayford, lecture.

NOTES

Chapter 2: Three Big Warning Signs
1. For example, see 1 John 3:4–9 and 1 John 5:16–18.

Chapter 3: Beware the Chaldeans
1. Walter A. Elwell and Philip W. Comfort, *Tyndale Bible Dictionary* (Wheaton, IL: Tyndale House, 2001): "The name of a land, and its inhabitants, in S Babylonia, later used to denote Babylonia as a whole, especially during the last dynasty of Babylonia (626–539 BC)."
2. Stelman Smith and Judson Cornwall, *The Exhaustive Dictionary of Bible Names* (North Brunswick, NJ: Bridge-Logos, 1998): Chaldeans #3.
3. For example, see John 10:11–12.
4. Charles Caldwell Ryrie, "The Doctrine of Satan" and "The Doctrine of Demons," in *The Ryrie Study Bible* (Chicago: Moody Bible Institute, 1978), 1943–46.
5. James Strong, *Enhanced Strong's Lexicon* (Bellingham, WA: Logos Bible Software, 2001): 3180, from a compound of 3326 and 3593 [cf "method"].
6. Ibid: 1080, *bâla*, corresponding to 1086 (used only in a mental sense).

Chapter 4: Breaking the Snare of Pride
1. See Mark 15:16.

Chapter 5: Breaking the Snare of Bitterness
1. James Strong, *Enhanced Strong's Lexicon* (Bellingham, WA: Logos Bible Software, 2001): 3392, *miaino*, "to dye with another colour, to stain."

Chapter 6: Breaking the Snare of Greed
1. Please note that there are many godly churches that pass an offering plate as a regular part of their weekend services. They use this method carefully and not for dishonest gain, and I don't mean to malign them or this method in any way.
2. Note that the book of Proverbs provides God-given general principles for wise living rather than specific commands. Yet the principle of firstfruits as a specific command is definitely found elsewhere in Scripture. See Exodus 13:2; Leviticus 23:10–14; Numbers 18:12; 2 Chronicles 31:5; Ezekiel 44:30; Nehemiah 10:35; Romans 11:16; and more.

Chapter 7: Breaking the Snare of Lust
1. James Strong, *Enhanced Strong's Lexicon* (Bellingham, WA: Logos Bible Software, 2001): 1939.

Chapter 8: Breaking the Snares in Your Mind

1. I am indebted to Jimmy Evans, author and CEO of the Dallas-based ministry Marriage Today, for his teaching on this subject. Jimmy's book *A Mind Set Free: Overcoming Mental Strongholds Through Biblical Meditation* (Amarillo, TX: Majestic Media Resources, 2000, 2004) provides an excellent resource for anyone seeking further study.
2. James Strong, *Enhanced Strong's Lexicon* (Bellingham, WA: Logos Bible Software, 2001): 163, from 164, *aichmalotos*.
3. Johannes P. Louw and Eugene Nida, *Greek-English Lexicon of the New Testament Based on Semantic Domains*, Logos Bible Software (New York: United Bible Societies, 1996): 3615.

Chapter 9: Breaking the Snares of Past Wounds

1. James Strong, *Enhanced Strong's Lexicon* (Bellingham, WA: Logos Bible Software, 2001): 4937.
2. Ibid: 2588.

Chapter 10: A Prayer for Freedom

1. James Strong, *Enhanced Strong's Lexicon* (Bellingham, WA: Logos Bible Software, 2001): 3326.
2. Ibid: 3341.
3. Johannes P. Louw and Eugene Nida, *Greek-English Lexicon of the New Testament Based on Semantic Domains*, Logos Bible Software (New York: United Bible Societies, 1996): 41.52.
4. Strong, *Enhanced Strong's Lexicon*: 2390, *iaomai*.

ABOUT THE AUTHOR

Robert Morris is the founding senior pastor of Gateway Church, a multicampus church in the Dallas–Fort Worth Metroplex. Since it began in 2000, Gateway has grown to more than thirty-six thousand active members.

Robert is featured on the weekly television program *The Blessed Life*, seen in one hundred million homes in the United States and in more than two hundred countries around the world.

Robert holds a doctorate of literature and serves as chairman of the board of the King's University.

He is the bestselling author of eleven books, including *The Blessed Life*, *The Blessed Church*, and *The God I Never Knew*.

Robert and his wife, Debbie, have been married more than thirty-five years. They have three married children and six grandchildren.

BREAK FREE!

IN THIS SIX-SESSION VIDEO-BASED STUDY, BESTSELLING author Robert Morris invites us into this glorious truth: the promise of being set free from sin is a promise to be set free completely. Although evil is real and Christians can be oppressed by it, we have the promise that the One who is in us is greater than the one who is in the world (1 John 4:4). Jesus saves us, trains us to resist the power of evil, and delivers us from anything that holds us back. With Jesus, we can be truly free forever.

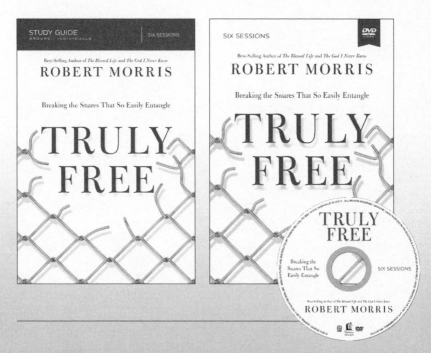

W PUBLISHING GROUP

AN IMPRINT OF THOMAS NELSON

FOR VIDEOS, SAMPLE CHAPTERS, AND OTHER *TRULY FREE* RESOURCES, VISIT TRULYFREEBOOK.COM